Maya and Ben

Teacher's Guide

Unit 1

Review

Note: See New and Important Objectives on page 2 for a complete list of skills taught and reviewed.

Critical Foundations in Primary Reading

Marilyn Sprick, Ann Watanabe, Karen Akiyama-Paik, and Shelley V. Jones

Sopris West®
EDUCATIONAL SERVICES
A Cambium Learning®Company

BOSTON, MA · LONGMONT, CO

ISBN 13-digit: 978-1-60218-524-1
ISBN 10-digit: 1-60218-524-7

7 8 9 10 11   B&B   16 15 14 13 12

166844/6-12

Table of Contents
Unit 1
Maya and Ben

Table of Contents

Letter Sounds and Combinations

Cumulative Review of *Read Well 1* Sounds and Combinations (Ss, Ee, ee, Mm, Aa, Dd, th, Nn, Tt, Ww, Ii, Th, Hh, Cc, Rr, ea, sh, Sh, Kk, -ck, oo, ar, wh, Wh, ĕ, -y as in fly, Ll, Oo, Bb, all, Gg, Ff, Uu, er, oo as in book, Yy, a schwa, Pp, ay, Vv, Qq, Jj, Xx, or, Zz, a_e, -y as in baby, i_e, ou, ow as in cow, ch, Ch, ai, igh, o_e, ir) and:

Unit 2	Unit 3	Unit 3	Unit 3	Unit 5	Unit 6
aw	**ew**	**ue**	**u_e**	**ow**	**ge**
/aw/	/ōō/	/ōō/	/ōō/	/ōōō/	/j/
P<u>aw</u>	Cr<u>ew</u>	Bl<u>ue</u>	Fl<u>u</u>t<u>e</u>	Sn<u>ow</u>	Pa<u>ge</u>
Voiced	Voiced	Voiced	Bossy <u>E</u> Voiced	Voiced (Long)	Voiced

Unit 6	Unit 7	Unit 7	Unit 8	Unit 8	Unit 10
-dge	**ci**	**ce**	**kn**	**ph**	**oa**
/j/	/sss/	/sss/	/nnn/	/fff/	/ōōō/
Ba<u>dge</u>	<u>Ci</u>rcle	<u>Ce</u>nter	<u>Kn</u>ee	<u>Ph</u>one	B<u>oa</u>t
Voiced	Unvoiced	Unvoiced	Voiced	Unvoiced	Voiced (Long)

Unit 11	Unit 11	Unit 12	Unit 12	Unit 13
oi	**ea**	**gi**	**au**	**oy**
/oi/	/ĕĕĕ/	/j/	/au/	/oy/
P<u>oi</u>nt	Br<u>ea</u>d	<u>Gi</u>raffe	Astron<u>au</u>t	B<u>oy</u>
Voiced	Voiced (Short)	Voiced	Voiced	Voiced

Affixes (including morphographs—affixes taught with meaning) and Open Syllables

Cumulative Review of *Read Well 1* Affixes (-ed, -en, -es, -ing, -ly, -s, -y, -tion) and:

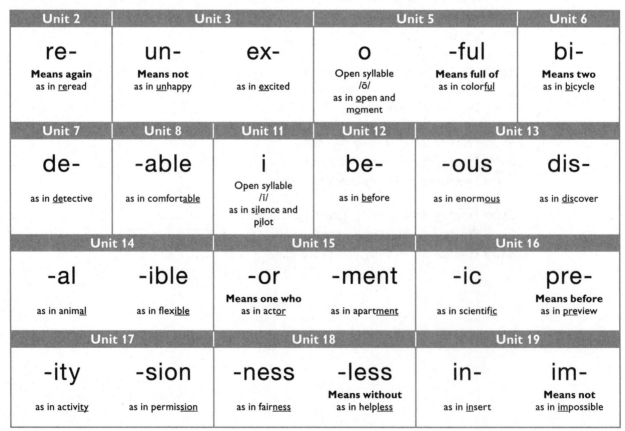

Unit 2	Unit 3	Unit 3	Unit 5	Unit 5	Unit 6
re-	**un-**	**ex-**	**o**	**-ful**	**bi-**
Means again	**Means not**		Open syllable /ō/	**Means full of**	**Means two**
as in <u>re</u>read	as in <u>un</u>happy	as in <u>ex</u>cited	as in <u>o</u>pen and m<u>o</u>ment	as in color<u>ful</u>	as in <u>bi</u>cycle

Unit 7	Unit 8	Unit 11	Unit 12	Unit 13	Unit 13
de-	**-able**	**i**	**be-**	**-ous**	**dis-**
		Open syllable /ī/			
as in <u>de</u>tective	as in comfort<u>able</u>	as in s<u>i</u>lence and p<u>i</u>lot	as in <u>be</u>fore	as in enorm<u>ous</u>	as in <u>dis</u>cover

Unit 14	Unit 14	Unit 15	Unit 15	Unit 16	Unit 16
-al	**-ible**	**-or**	**-ment**	**-ic**	**pre-**
		Means one who			**Means before**
as in anim<u>al</u>	as in flex<u>ible</u>	as in act<u>or</u>	as in apart<u>ment</u>	as in scientif<u>ic</u>	as in <u>pre</u>view

Unit 17	Unit 17	Unit 18	Unit 18	Unit 19	Unit 19
-ity	**-sion**	**-ness**	**-less**	**in-**	**im-**
			Means without		**Means not**
as in activ<u>ity</u>	as in permi<u>ssion</u>	as in fair<u>ness</u>	as in help<u>less</u>	as in <u>in</u>sert	as in <u>im</u>possible

Introduction
Maya and Ben

Story Notes

The theme of the first storybook is *Our World, Our Home.* The first unit starts in the Bronx, home to second grade students Maya and Ben.

A Perfect Year: Maya and Ben learn to work through their differences. It's a perfect year for Maya until a funny kid with spiky hair shows up. What's a person to think when a kid named Benjamin Franklin Thomas Edison Wright sits right next to you?

Eel in the Fish Tank: Second grade from the point of view of the classroom pet.

Recommended Read Aloud

The *Read Well 2* suggested Read Alouds enhance small group instruction—providing opportunities to further build background knowledge and vocabulary.

CAUTION (Reminder)
Do not read the Read Aloud recommendations during small group instruction. Reserve this time for students to read.

Enemy Pie by Derek Munson
Fiction • Narrative

The summer was perfect until Jeremy Ross moved in down the street. Fortunately, Dad has the recipe for Enemy Pie, a surefire way to get rid of enemies. One of its secret ingredients is spending the entire day playing with the enemy! Students will enjoy this sweet lesson on how to turn your worst enemy into your best friend.

Read Well Connections

Just when everything seems perfect, something comes along to change things. In both stories, students read about the difficulties and rewards of making new friends and welcoming new students and neighbors.

NOTE FROM THE AUTHORS

USING VOCABULARY

Your enthusiasm for new words will help students build their speaking vocabulary.

Write new words on the board. Keep a running list of words you would like to remind yourself to use. Encourage students to use the words throughout the day in natural contexts.

New and Important Objectives
A Research-Based Reading Program

Phonemic Awareness
Phonics
Fluency
Vocabulary
Comprehension

Phonological and Phonemic Awareness

Segmenting, Blending; Rhyming; Onset and Rime;
Counting Syllables

Phonics

Cumulative Letter Sounds and Combinations

Review • Ss, Ee, ee, Mm, Aa, Dd, th, Nn, Tt, Ww, Ii, Th, Hh,
Cc, Rr, ea, sh, Sh, Kk, -ck, oo, ar, wh, Wh, ĕ, -y (as in fly), Ll,
Oo, Bb, all, Gg, Ff, Uu, er, oo (as in book), Yy, a (schwa), Pp,
ay, Vv, Qq, Jj, Xx, or, Zz, a_e, -y (as in baby), i_e, ou, ow (as in
cow), ch, Ch, ai, igh, o_e, ir

Cumulative Affixes and Morphographs

Review • -ed, -en, -er, -es, -est, -ing, -ly, -s, -y, -tion

☆New Abbreviations

a.m., Mr., p.m.

☆New Contractions

he's, we're

☆New Proper Nouns

Ana, Ana's, Ben's, Benjamin Franklin Thomas Edison
Wright, Bronx, Jones, Maya Martinez, Maya's, Mr. Chapman,
Mr. Chapman's, North America, Saturday, United States,
Wednesday

---

* **Known Pattern Words With Affixes** and **Known Tricky Words With Affixes** have base words students have previously read.
The words are new in this unit because they have not been previously read with the affix.

☆ = New in this unit

Phonics (continued)

★New Pattern Words

band, bead, beads, bend, blurt, blurted, bond, bound, bounding, braid, braided, care, chair, check, cheese, class, couch, crowd, crowded, desk, draw, drums, dusk, eel, for, gave, glare, glaring, grade, hang, here, howl, hung, kind, main, map, maps, mouth, much, munch, munched, our, painted, plain, playing, pout, pouting, round, scare, scared, scowl, scowled, scowls, scratch, scratched, screen, sigh, sighed, slime, spike, starve, starved, stuff, taps, tug, tugged, turn, turned, type, typed, use, used, web

*Known Pattern Words With Affixes • buzzed, chips, dropped, ended, feeder, feeds, helped, hoped, kicker, plays, sticks, stopping, teaching, zoomed, zooming

★New Compound and Hyphenated Words

anywhere, classroom, doorbell, downstairs, everything, myself, playground, underline, understands, whoever, without

★Other New Multisyllabic Words

address, almost, amaze, amazed, amazing, amount, appeared, apples, camera, compute, computer, computers, continent, crayons, describe, dribble, exactly, exclaimed, family, forgot, hesitate, hesitated, important, inventor, inventors, mighty, moody, open, opened, ordinary, over, project, projects, respect, shuffled, slimy, soccer, spiky, tardy

★New Tricky Words

banana, carried, carry, city, country, hey, hi, idea, oh, ordinary, page, picture, pull, pulled, science, scientist, sorry, talk, talks, thought, through, worse

*Known Tricky Words With Affixes • doing, moved, walked

Fluency

Accuracy, Expression, Phrasing, Rate

Vocabulary

New • amazed, inventor, perfect, plain, pout, respect, scowl, speechless

Review • ordinary

Reviewed in Context • hesitate, ordinary

Idioms and Expressions

New • get carried away

Comprehension

Unit Genres
Fiction • Realistic Narrative
Fiction • Imaginative

Comprehension Processes
Build Knowledge: Factual, Procedural, Conceptual

Day	1	2	3	4	5	6
Remember						
Defining						
Identifying (recalling)	S,C	S,C	S,C	C	S,C	C
Using		C				
Understand						
Defining (in your own words)	S		S,C		S	
Describing	C		S		S,C	
Explaining (rephrasing)	S	S,C	S,C	S	S,C	
Illustrating			C			
Sequencing					C	
Summarizing		S		S	S,C	
Using	S,C	S,C	S,C	S,C	S,C	
Visualizing						
Apply						
Demonstrating	S		S			
Explaining (unstated)	S,C	S		S	S	
Illustrating						
Inferring	S,C	S	S,C	S,C	S	C
Making Connections (relating)	S		S			
Predicting	S	S	S	S	S	
Using	S	S	S		S	
Analyze						
Classifying						
Comparing/Contrasting					S	
Distinguishing Cause/Effect						
Drawing Conclusions		S				
Inferring		S				
Evaluate						
Making Judgments						
Responding (personal)						
Create						
Generating Ideas						

E = Exercise, S = Storybook, C = Comprehension & Skill

Comprehension (continued)

Skills and Strategies

Day	1	2	3	4	5	6
Priming Background Knowledge						
Setting a Purpose for Reading						
Answering Questions	S	S	S	S	S	
Asking Questions						
Visualizing						
Comprehension Monitoring/Fix Ups						
Does it Make Sense?	C	C	C	E,C	C	C
Looking Back						
Restating						
Summarizing						
Main Idea						
Retelling						
Supporting Details						
Understanding Text Structure						
Title, Author, Illustrator	S	S	S		S	
Fact or Fiction						
Genre (Classifying)						
Narrative						
Setting	C		C	C	S,C	
Main Character/Traits (Characterization)*	S,C	S,C	S,C	C	S,C	C
Goal				C		
Problem/Solution	S	S	S			
Action/Events/Sequence	S			S	S,C	C
Outcome/Conclusion						
Lesson/Author's Message						
Expository						
Subject/Topic						
Heading						
Supporting Details (Facts/Information)						
Main Idea	C					C
Using Graphic Organizers						
Chart						
Diagram (labeling)						
Hierarchy (topic/detail)						
K-W-L						
Map (locating, labeling)						
Matrix (compare/contrast)						
Sequence (linear, cycle, cause and effect)						
Story Map					C	
Web					C	

E = Exercise, S = Storybook, C = Comprehension & Skill

*Narrator

Comprehension (continued)

Study Skills

Day	1	2	3	4	5	6
Alphabetical Order			C			
Following Directions						C
Locating Information						
Note Taking						
Previewing						
Reviewing						
Test Taking						
Using Glossary						
Using Table of Contents	S					C
Viewing	S,C			S		
Verifying						

Writing in Response to Reading

Day	1	2	3	4	5	6
Sentence Completion	C		C		C	C
Making Lists						
Sentence Writing	C		C	C		C
Story Retell/Summary					C	
Fact Summary						
Paragraph Writing						
Report Writing						
Open-Ended Response						
Creative Writing						

Writing Traits

(Addressed within the context of Writing in Response to Reading)

Day	1	2	3	4	5	6
Ideas and Content						
Elaborating/Generating						
Organization						
Introduction						
Topic Sentence						
Supporting Details						
Sequencing						
Word Choice						
Sophisticated Words (Tier 2 and 3)						
Conventions						
Capital	C		C		C	C
Ending Punctuation	C	C	C	C	C	C
Other (commas, quotation marks)						
Presentation						
Handwriting						
Neatness						

E = Exercise, S = Storybook, C = Comprehension & Skill

Daily Lesson Planning

LESSON PLAN FORMAT

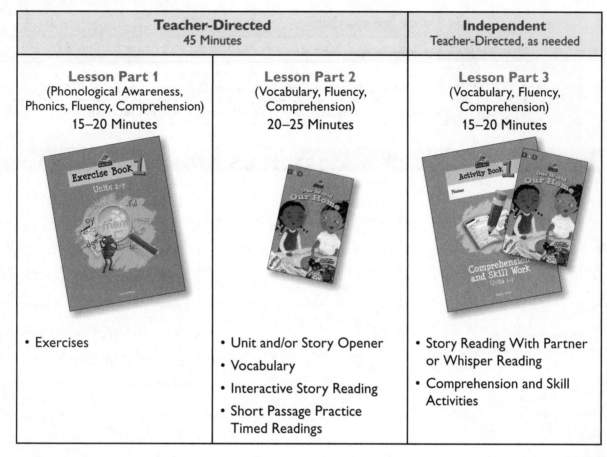

Teacher-Directed 45 Minutes		Independent Teacher-Directed, as needed
Lesson Part 1 (Phonological Awareness, Phonics, Fluency, Comprehension) 15–20 Minutes	**Lesson Part 2** (Vocabulary, Fluency, Comprehension) 20–25 Minutes	**Lesson Part 3** (Vocabulary, Fluency, Comprehension) 15–20 Minutes
• Exercises	• Unit and/or Story Opener • Vocabulary • Interactive Story Reading • Short Passage Practice Timed Readings	• Story Reading With Partner or Whisper Reading • Comprehension and Skill Activities

HOMEWORK

Read Well Homework (blackline masters of new *Read Well 2* passages) provides an opportunity for children to celebrate accomplishments with parents. Homework should be sent home on routine days.

ORAL READING FLUENCY ASSESSMENT

Upon completion of this unit, assess each student and proceed to Unit 2, as appropriate.

Note: See Making Decisions for additional assessment information.

DIFFERENTIATED LESSON PLANS

The differentiated lesson plans illustrate how to use materials for students with various learning needs. As you set up your unit plan, always include *Read Well 2* Exercises and Story Reading on a daily basis. Unit 1 includes 6-, 8-, 9-, 10-, and 11-Day Plans.

Plans	For groups that:
6-DAY	Complete Oral Reading Fluency Assessments with Passes and Strong Passes
8-DAY	Complete Oral Reading Fluency Assessments with Passes and require teacher-guided assistance with Story Reading and Comprehension and Skill Work
9-, 10-, or 11-DAY	Have difficulty passing the unit Oral Reading Fluency Assessments

6-DAY PLAN

Day 1

Teacher-Directed
- Exercise 1
- Unit and Story Opener: Maya and Ben; A Perfect Year
- Vocabulary, Ch. 1, 2
- A Perfect Year, Ch. 1
- Guide practice, as needed, on Comp & Skill 1, 2

Independent Work
- Repeated Reading: Partner or Whisper Read, A Perfect Year, Ch. 1
- Comp & Skill 1, 2

Homework
- Homework Passage 1

Day 2

Teacher-Directed
- Exercise 2
- A Perfect Year, Ch. 2
- Guide practice, as needed, on Comp & Skill 3, 4

Independent Work
- Repeated Reading: Partner or Whisper Read, A Perfect Year, Ch. 2
- Comp & Skill 3, 4

Homework
- Homework Passage 2

Day 3

Teacher-Directed
- Exercise 3
- Vocabulary, Ch. 3, 4
- A Perfect Year, Ch. 3
- Guide practice, as needed, on Comp & Skill 5, 6

Independent Work
- Repeated Reading: Partner or Whisper Read, A Perfect Year, Ch. 3
- Comp & Skill 5, 6

Homework
- Homework Passage 3

Day 4

Teacher-Directed
- Exercise 4a
- Exercise 4b: Focus Lesson
- A Perfect Year, Ch. 4
- Guide practice, as needed, on Comp & Skill 7, 8

Independent Work
- Repeated Reading: Partner or Whisper Read, A Perfect Year, Ch. 4
- Comp & Skill 7, 8

Homework
- Homework Passage 4

Day 5

Teacher-Directed
- Exercise 5
- Vocabulary, Ch. 5
- A Perfect Year, Ch. 5
- Guide practice, as needed, on Comp & Skill 9, 10

Independent Work
- Repeated Reading: Partner or Whisper Read, A Perfect Year, Ch. 5
- Comp & Skill 9, 10

Homework
- Homework Passage 5

Day 6

Teacher-Directed
- Exercise 6
- Fluency, Eel in the Fish Tank
- Guide practice, as needed, on Comp & Skill 11, 12

Independent Work
- Repeated Reading: Partner or Whisper Read, Eel in the Fish Tank
- Comp & Skill 11, 12
- Oral Reading Fluency Assessment

Homework
- Homework Passage 6

8-DAY PLAN • *Pre-Intervention*

Day 1

Teacher-Directed
- Exercise 1
- Unit and Story Opener: Maya and Ben; A Perfect Year
- Vocabulary, Ch. 1, 2
- A Perfect Year, Ch. 1
- Guide practice, as needed, on Comp & Skill 1

Independent Work
- Repeated Reading: Partner or Whisper Read, A Perfect Year, Ch. 1
- Comp & Skill 1

Homework
- Homework Passage 1

Day 2

Teacher-Directed
- Review Exercise 1
- Review Vocabulary, Ch. 1, 2
- Reread A Perfect Year, Ch. 1
- Guide practice, as needed, on Comp & Skill 2

Independent Work
- Repeated Reading: Partner or Whisper Read, A Perfect Year, Ch. 1
- Comp & Skill 2

Homework
- Extra Practice Word Fluency A

Day 3

Teacher-Directed
- Exercise 2
- A Perfect Year, Ch. 2
- Guide practice, as needed, on Comp & Skill 3, 4

Independent Work
- Repeated Reading: Partner or Whisper Read, A Perfect Year, Ch. 2
- Comp & Skill 3, 4

Homework
- Homework Passage 2

Day 4

Teacher-Directed
- Exercise 3
- Vocabulary, Ch. 3, 4
- A Perfect Year, Ch. 3
- Guide practice, as needed, on Comp & Skill 5

Independent Work
- Repeated Reading: Partner or Whisper Read, A Perfect Year, Ch. 3
- Comp & Skill 5

Homework
- Homework Passage 3

Day 5

Teacher-Directed
- Review Exercise 3
- Review Vocabulary, Ch. 3, 4
- Reread A Perfect Year, Ch. 3
- Guide practice, as needed, on Comp & Skill 6

Independent Work
- Repeated Reading: Partner or Whisper Read, A Perfect Year, Ch. 3
- Comp & Skill 6

Homework
- Comp & Skill 3 (Fluency Passage)

Day 6

Teacher-Directed
- Exercise 4a
- Exercise 4b: Focus Lesson
- A Perfect Year, Ch. 4
- Guide practice, as needed, on Comp & Skill 7, 8

Independent Work
- Repeated Reading: Partner or Whisper Read, A Perfect Year, Ch. 4
- Comp & Skill 7, 8

Homework
- Homework Passage 4

Day 7

Teacher-Directed
- Exercise 5
- Vocabulary, Ch. 5
- A Perfect Year, Ch. 5
- Guide practice, as needed, on Comp & Skill 9, 10

Independent Work
- Repeated Reading: Partner or Whisper Read, A Perfect Year, Ch. 5
- Comp & Skill 9, 10

Homework
- Homework Passage 5

Day 8

Teacher-Directed
- Exercise 6
- Fluency, Eel in the Fish Tank
- Guide practice, as needed, on Comp & Skill 11, 12

Independent Work
- Repeated Reading: Partner or Whisper Read, Eel in the Fish Tank
- Comp & Skill 11, 12
- Oral Reading Fluency Assessment

Homework
- Homework Passage 6

9-, 10-, or 11-DAY PLAN • *Intervention*
For Days 1–8, follow 8-Day plan. Add Days 9, 10, 11 as follows:

Day 9 Extra Practice 1

Teacher-Directed
- Decoding Practice
- Fluency Passage

Independent Work
- Activity and Word Fluency A

Homework
- Fluency Passage

Day 10 Extra Practice 2

Teacher-Directed
- Decoding Practice
- Fluency Passage

Independent Work
- Activity and Word Fluency B

Homework
- Fluency Passage

Day 11 Extra Practice 3

Teacher-Directed
- Decoding Practice
- Fluency Passage

Independent Work
- Activity and Word Fluency A or B
- Oral Reading Fluency Assessment

Homework
- Fluency Passage

Materials and Materials Preparation

Core Lessons

Teacher Materials

READ WELL 2 MATERIALS

- Unit 1 Teacher's Guide
- Sound Cards
- Unit 1 Oral Reading Fluency Assessment found on page 79
- Group Assessment Record found in the *Assessment Manual*

SCHOOL SUPPLIES

Stopwatch or watch with a second hand

Student Materials

READ WELL 2 MATERIALS (for each student)

- *Our World, Our Home* storybook
- *Exercise Book 1*
- *Activity Book 1* or copies of Unit 1 Comprehension and Skill Work
- Unit 1 Certificate of Achievement (BLM, page 80)
- Unit 1 Goal Setting (BLM, page 81)
- Unit 1 Homework (blackline masters)
  See *Getting Started* for suggested homework routines.

SCHOOL SUPPLIES

Pencils, colors (optional—markers, crayons, or colored pencils)

> Make one copy per student of each blackline master, as appropriate for the group.
>
> *Note:* For new or difficult Comprehension and Skill Activities, make overhead transparencies from the blackline masters. Use the transparencies to demonstrate and guide practice.

Extra Practice Lessons

> **CAUTION**
> Use these lessons only if needed. Students who need Extra Practice may benefit from one, two, or three lessons.

> **FOCUS LESSONS**
> For Exercise 4b (Focus Lesson), make overhead transparencies from the blackline masters, write on transparencies placed over the pages, or use paper copies to demonstrate how to complete the lessons.

Student Materials

READ WELL 2 MATERIALS (for each student, as needed)

See Extra Practice Blackline Masters located on the CD.

- Unit 1 Extra Practice 1: Decoding Practice, Fluency Passage, Word Fluency A, and Activity
- Unit 1 Extra Practice 2: Decoding Practice, Fluency Passage, Word Fluency B, and Activity
- Unit 1 Extra Practice 3: Decoding Practice, Fluency Passage, Word Fluency A or B, and Activity

SCHOOL SUPPLIES

Pencils, colors (markers, crayons, or colored pencils), highlighters

Important Tips

Explicit Teaching
Teaching to Mastery: Decoding Errors
Expectations for Written Work
Working With English Language Learners

Explicit Teaching

PRINCIPLES OF EXPLICIT INSTRUCTION

Apply the steps of explicit instruction to the careful programming in *Read Well 2* and your students will achieve high levels of success. Use the steps of explicit instruction, as appropriate.

- **Demonstrate.**
  Show or model a skill or strategy.
  Say things like: My turn. Watch me.

- **Guide.**
  Practice the skill or strategy with students.
  Say things like: Our turn. Say it with me. Let's . . .

- **Provide opportunities for independent practice.**
  Mix group and individual turns, independent of your voice or action.
  Say things like: Your turn. I'll listen. I'll watch . . .

- **Provide gentle, supportive corrections.**
  Attain mastery through the use of gentle, supportive group corrections. For every error, reteach with demonstration and guided practice.

  Go on to another task, but come back to the difficult skill for at least three correct and independent responses. Give an individual turn to any student who had difficulty initially.

- **Acknowledge student efforts and accomplishments.**
  Provide positive and descriptive feedback.
  Say things like: Meg, you read each syllable in that big word. Excellent.

WHEN APPROPRIATE

Knowing when to demonstrate, guide practice, and provide independent practice is an art. Watch your students. Listen carefully, then use the steps of explicit instruction judiciously.

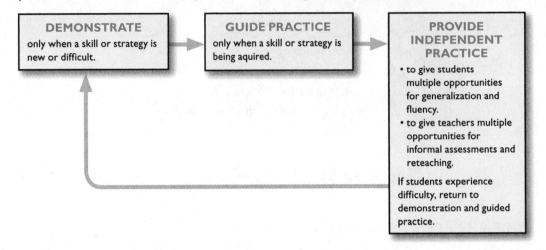

DEMONSTRATE
only when a skill or strategy is new or difficult.

GUIDE PRACTICE
only when a skill or strategy is being aquired.

PROVIDE INDEPENDENT PRACTICE
- to give students multiple opportunities for generalization and fluency.
- to give teachers multiple opportunities for informal assessments and reteaching.

If students experience difficulty, return to demonstration and guided practice.

The goal of explicit instruction is independence.

Teaching to Mastery: Decoding Errors

When a student or students make decoding errors in the Exercises, *provide gentle group corrections.*

SHIFTY WORD BLENDING

Error: Students do not sound out smoothly.

- Provide descriptive feedback. Say something like:
  I heard Bumpy Blending: /sh/ • /ou/ • /t/.

- Demonstrate sounding out the word "shout" smoothly.
  If you sound out smoothly, your reading will sound like we talk.
  Listen to me sound out smoothly.
  I won't stop between the sounds. /shshshououout/
  Tell me the word. (shout)
  If we blend smoothly, we can sound out a word in a sentence, and it will still sound good. Listen: We can /shshshououout/ on the playground.
  What can we do? (shout on the playground)

- Guide sounding out smoothly.
  Let's sound out smoothly. /shshshououout/ Tell me the word. (shout)

- Repeat, mixing group and individual turns, independent of your voice.
  Sound out smoothly by yourselves. (/shshshououout/)
  Tell me the word. (shout)

> **BUILDING MASTERY**
> - Write any misidentified word on the board.
> - Follow the correction procedures.
> - Review the words at the end of the lesson.

Critical Step ▶
- Practice other examples.
  Return to the difficult word at least three times.
- Acknowledge student efforts.

SOUND

Error: A student or students read "plan" for "plain."

- Have students identify the missed sound.
  There was one sound that tricked some of us.
  Point to the sound. Tell me the sound. (/āāā/)

Have students correct the error. ▶
- Have students sound out the word with the correct sound.
  Sound out the word smoothly. (plllāāānnn) Read the word. (plain) The opposite of fancy is . . . (plain). That's right. That hat is not fancy. It is . . . plain.

- Practice other words. Return to the difficult word at least three times.
Critical Step ▶
- Acknowledge student responses. You know the difference between *plan* and *plain*.

WORD PART

Error: A student or students read "understand" for "underline."

- Have students identify the missed word part. There was one word part that tricked some of us.
  Point to the word part. Tell me the word part. (line)

- Have students say the word by parts with the correct word part. Loop under each part.
  Read the word by parts. (un-der-line)
  Read the word. (underline) When you draw a line under something, you . . . underline.

- Practice other words. Return to the difficult word at least three times.
- Acknowledge student responses. Great! You didn't let the multisyllabic word fool you.

Expectations for Written Work

HIGH EXPECTATIONS

Maintain high expectations not only for teacher-directed lessons in decoding and comprehension, but also for independent written work.

TEACH EXPECTATIONS FOR WRITTEN WORK

Just as students are taught procedures for behavioral expectations, written work expectations must also be taught.

If you expect it, you must teach it.

Explain and model the expectation and verify students' understanding with positive and negative examples.

It is important to do your best on your Comprehension and Skill Work.

You always want to be proud of your efforts.

Doing your best means that you work carefully and check to make sure you do the following:

1. Keep your paper flat, whole, and neat.

What should your paper look like? (flat, whole, and neat)

First, your paper should be flat.

Show examples of a flat and crumpled paper.

Point to the paper that is best.

Next, your paper should be whole.

Show examples of a whole paper and a torn paper.

Point to the paper that is best.

Your paper should be neat, without extra marks.

Show examples of a paper with scribbles and one without scribbles.

Point to the paper that is best.

> I'll put myself to the test.
> I'll do my very best.
>
> I'll keep my paper flat.
> I'll do it just like that.
>
> I'll keep my paper whole.
> Oh, what a goal!
>
> I'll keep my paper neat.
> My writing can't be beat.
>
> I'll put myself to the test.
> I'll always do my best.

2. Your next job is to write as neatly as you can.

Everyone will have a personal best in handwriting.

Let's look at two of my papers. I worked carefully on one and not the other.

Project two examples—an example of your personal best and a non-example.

Have your students vote. Which paper do you think is the best?

This one? Or this one?

This is my personal best because the letters sit on the lines.

The letters are formed correctly, and I have spaces between the words.

3. Use capitals at the beginning of sentences and periods at the end of sentences.

4. Have students practice.

Have students practice writing an answer to a written question.

5. Provide gentle, supportive corrections.

6. Acknowledge students' efforts and accomplishments.

Provide each student with a sample of his or her own personal best to use as a reference.

[Jonelle], you left a space between every word. Excellent. This paper goes in your folder as a sample of your personal best!

Using Assessment Results

ORAL READING FLUENCY (ORF) ASSESSMENTS

Starting with Unit 1, End-of-Unit Oral Reading Fluency Assessments assess students' ability to read new words in the context of an oral reading passage.

USING ORF ASSESSMENT RESULTS

With *Read Well,* every teacher is a diagnostician. The assessment scores will allow you to:

- analyze the strengths and weaknesses of a group of students.

- compare the progress of individual students with group progress.

- quickly share assessment results with colleagues.

- make regrouping decisions.

*Every **Read Well** teacher is a diagnostician.*

You are a diagnostician. Review each child's assessment results to make instructional decisions.

- Look at the level at which the student passed (Strong Pass, Pass, No Pass).

- Determine error patterns and reteach any difficult words or skills.

- Plan to make adjustments in your plans.
  Provide systematic review and Extra Practice, as needed.

- Make necessary adjustments in grouping.

STRONG PASS

Consistent Strong Passes signal the possibility of moving faster. Significantly higher fluency scores for one or more students may indicate the need to regroup.

PASS

A Pass signals an appropriate pace of instruction.

NO PASS

A No Pass indicates the need for immediate reteaching, possible intervention, and regrouping.

Teach, Assess, Adjust
Teach, Assess, Adjust
Teach, Assess, Adjust

Working With English Language Learners

When English Language Learners (ELLs) are placed appropriately in *Read Well*, they receive instruction that aligns with research-based recommendations. (See *Getting Started* pages 32 to 35.) Because ELLs face additional challenges, increase the intensity and amount of instruction by augmenting an English oral language program with extra *Read Well* instruction.

WHAT RESEARCH SUGGESTS

The Institute of Education Sciences National Center for Education Evaluation and Regional Assistance reviewed research on ELLs and reported its findings in *Effective Literacy and English Language Instruction for English Learners in the Elementary Grades*. The committee's recommendations for improving reading and language of ELLs are shown in the table below.

◆◆ ELL RECOMMENDATION Level of Evidence: Strong	Recommendation	Enhancements
	1. Formative Assessments	No enhancements necessary.
	2. Focused, Intensive Small Group Intervention	Double Dose of *Read Well* instruction for ELLs • If fluency scores are low, preteach a balanced lesson to include: Exercises, selected Vocabulary, Story Reading, and Comprehension and Skill Work. • If fluency scores are strong, preteach selected vocabulary and Story Reading, and orally practice how to complete written work.
	3. Vocabulary Instruction Throughout the Day	Encourage students to use vocabulary words. Assist with understanding of words. Demonstrate and guide how to speak in complete sentences.
	4. Peer-Assisted Learning	Regular Lesson • Include Partner Reading. • Include Partner Think and Talk (starting with Unit 9). Periodically have ELLs start first. Double Dose • Discuss selected gray text questions in partners and then with the group. • Preteach selected Comprehension and Skill Work by having students orally discuss answers.
◆◆ ELL RECOMMENDATION Level of Evidence: Low (Adequate research is needed for evidence to be considered Strong.)	5. Development of Academic English	• Teach students how to respond in complete thoughts. Demonstrate or model, guide, then have students respond, independent of your help. • When discussing the story, focus first on the central elements of the story—who the story is about, the problem and/or goal, the action, and the outcome. • Next, work on inferences. • Prompt complete sentence responses, as appropriate.

How to Teach the Lessons

Teach from this section. Each instructional component is outlined in an easy-to-teach format.

Exercise 1

- Unit and Story Opener: Ben and Maya; A Perfect Year
- Vocabulary
- Story Reading 1
  With the Teacher: Chapter 1
- Comprehension and Skill Activities 1, 2

Exercise 2

- Story Reading 2
  With the Teacher: Chapter 2
- Comprehension and Skill Activities 3, 4

Exercise 3

- Vocabulary
- Story Reading 3
  With the Teacher: Chapter 3
- Comprehension and Skill Activities 5, 6

Exercise 4a

- Exercise 4b: Focus Lesson
- Story Reading 4
  With the Teacher: Chapter 4
- Comprehension and Skill Activities 7, 8

Exercise 5

- Vocabulary
- Story Reading 5
  With the Teacher: Chapter 5
- Comprehension and Skill Activities 9, 10

Exercise 6

- Story Reading 6
  With the Teacher: Eel in the Fish Tank (Fluency)
- Comprehension and Skill Activities 11, 12

Note: Lessons include daily homework.

★❶ SOUND REVIEW

Have students read the sounds and key words. Work for accuracy, then fluency.

PACING

Exercise 1 should take about 15 minutes.

★❷ SHIFTY WORD BLENDING

For each word, have students say the underlined sound, sound out the word, and say it.

★❸ SOUND PRACTICE

- For each column, have students spell and say the focus sound in the gray bar.
  Next, have students read each underlined sound and the word, then read the whole column.
  Say something like: Look at the first gray bar. Spell, then say the sound.
  Listen: a̲-i̲ says /āāā/. Your turn. (a̲-i̲ says /āāā/)
  Now read each underlined sound, then the whole word.
  Listen: /āāā/, chair, /āāā/, braided . . . Your turn. (/āāā/, chair; /āāā/, braided; /āāā/, hair . . .)
  Now, go back to the top and read the whole words. (chair, braided, hair, main)
- Repeat with each column, building accuracy first, then fluency.

★❹ ACCURACY AND FLUENCY BUILDING

- For each task, have students say any underlined part, then read the word.
- Set a pace. Then have students read the whole words in each task and column.
- Provide repeated practice, building accuracy first, then fluency.

A2. Abbreviations

Tell students that abbreviations are a short way of writing a longer word or words.
Have students read each abbreviation. Say something like:
Abbreviations are a short way of writing a longer word. Read the first abbreviation. (a.m.)
The abbreviation *a.m.* means in the morning. I get up at 6:30 in the morning. I get up at 6:30 . . . a.m.

C1. Multisyllabic Words

- Introduce students to syllables.
  You can read big words called multisyllabic words. Each word part is a syllable.
- Have students read each syllable out loud, finger count the syllables, then read the word. Use the word in a sentence, as appropriate.

D1. Tricky Words

- For each Tricky Word, have students use the sounds and word parts they know to silently sound out the word. Use the word in a sentence to help with pronunciation. If the word is unfamiliar, tell students the word. Then have students say, spell, and say it.
  Use my sentence to help you pronounce the word. When you greet someone, you say . . . "Hi."
  Spell the word. (h̲-i̲) Read the word three times. (hi, hi, hi)

thought	Edie couldn't decide what to do. She asked what I . . . *thought*.
worse	This apple isn't as good as the one I ate yesterday. This one is . . . *worse*.
Wednesday	The day that comes after Tuesday is . . . *Wednesday*.
ordinary	Something that is not special is . . . *ordinary*.
science	Alyson wants to learn more about . . . *science*.
soccer	A game where you try to kick the ball into the goal is . . . *soccer*.
Ana	Jorge's sister is named . . . *Ana*.

- Have students go back and read the whole words in the column.

★❺ COMPOUND WORDS

Tell students that compound words have two small words in one big word.

★ = New in this unit

★❻ READING BY ANALOGY

Have students figure out how to say *re-* by reading other words they know. Say something like:
Read the first word. (me) Read the next word. (be) Read the next part. (re-) Look at the next
word. Read the underlined part, then the whole word. (re-, respect) Read the sentence. (I *respect*
people who work hard.)

A Perfect Year

Unit 1 Exercise 1
Use before Chapter 1

★1. SOUND REVIEW Have students review sounds for accuracy, then for fluency.

A	ĕ as in end	-y as in baby	o as in otter	i as in insect
B	igh u ir a ai ch ou			

★2. SHIFTY WORD BLENDING For each word, have students say the underlined part, sound out smoothly, then read the word.

d<u>e</u>sk	d<u>u</u>sk	du<u>ck</u>	<u>m</u>uck	mu<u>ch</u>

★3. SOUND PRACTICE In each column, have students spell and say the sound, then say any underlined sound and the word. Next, have students read the whole column.

ai	igh	u	ee	a as in ago
ch<u>ai</u>r	m<u>igh</u>ty	dr<u>u</u>ms	m<u>ee</u>t	<u>a</u>go
br<u>ai</u>ded	s<u>igh</u>ed	st<u>u</u>ff	<u>ee</u>l	M<u>a</u>ya
h<u>ai</u>r	Wr<u>igh</u>t	y<u>u</u>ck	n<u>ee</u>d	Benj<u>a</u>min
m<u>ai</u>n				Th<u>o</u>m<u>a</u>s

★4. ACCURACY AND FLUENCY BUILDING For each column, have students say any underlined part, then read each word. Next, have students read the whole column.

A1 Mixed Practice	B1 Word Endings	C1 Multisyllabic Words		D1 Tricky Words
grade	<u>doing</u>	Frank•lin	Franklin	hi
p<u>l</u>ays	<u>beads</u>	sec•ond	second	thought
tard<u>y</u>	<u>walked</u>	Ed•i•son	Edison	worse
ki<u>ck</u>er	going	Mar•tin•ez	Martinez	Wednesday
A2 Abbreviations	pla<u>y</u>ing	Chap•man	Chapman	ordinary
a.m.	spike	hap•pen	happen	science
Mr.	spiky	per•fect	perfect	soccer
p.m.				Ana

★5. COMPOUND WORDS Have students read each word part, then read each whole word.

A	my•self	myself	class•room	classroom
B	what•ever	whatever	every•thing	everything
C	play•ground	playground		

★6. READING BY ANALOGY Have students figure out the underlined part by reading other words they know.

me be re- <u>re</u>spect	I <u>re</u>spect people who work hard.

   1

TEAM EXPECTATIONS

Have students tell you the team expectations. Say something like:
Who can tell me the first two team rules?

1. Sit up.
2. Follow directions.
3. Help each other.
4. Work hard and have fun.

SILENT LETTERS

Tell students letters with slashes through them are silent. They don't say anything.

BUILD ACCURACY AND FLUENCY

For all rows and columns, follow the specific directions, then build accuracy and fluency with whole words.

COMPREHENSION PROCESSES

Remember, Understand, Apply

PROCEDURES

1. Introducing the Storybook and Theme

Identifying—Title; Viewing; Inferring; Using Table of Contents

• Tell students the title of their storybook is *Our World, Our Home.*
Say something like:

Everyone, look at the cover of the book.
What's the title of the book? (Our World, Our Home)

What do you see on the cover? (two kids)
Yes, and they look about your age.
What grade do you think they're in? (second, third)
What do you think they're doing? (art, making a poster, making a map of Earth . . .)

• Have students turn to the Table of Contents on page 3.
Say something like:

Now turn to page 3. This is called the Table of Contents. It tells the names of the units in the book and also the story and chapter titles.

Look on page 3. Unit 1 is called "Maya and Ben."

The first story title is in red. It's called "A Perfect Year." Touch under "A Perfect Year."

Turn to pages 4 and 5. Pages 4 and 5 show the Table of Contents for the next two units. We'll look more closely at those pages when we read Units 2 and 3.

Turn back to page 3. Read the title of the first story.
(A Perfect Year)
Follow the dotted line. Tell me the page that "A Perfect Year" begins on. (page 7)

Turn to page 7.

3

2. Using the Title Page and Introducing the Story

Identifying—Author; Explaining

• Discuss the title page.
Say something like:

Pages 6 and 7 open the unit.

Page 7 is the title page for the first story. Who is the author? (Ms. Mak)

Ms. Mak is short for the three authors who wrote this story together. Their names are Marilyn, Ann, and Karen. "Mak" is short for their names.

Under Ms. Mak, it says "illustrated by Jana Christy." What do you think Jana Christy did? (drew the pictures)

Yes, the illustrator is the person who drew the pictures for the story.

• Read and discuss the gray text questions.

A Perfect Year

by Ms. Mak
illustrated by Jana Christy

What is the title of the story?¹ If you could have a perfect year, what would it be like?²

7

❶ **Remember:** Identifying—Title (The title is "A Perfect Year.")

❷ **Apply:** Making Connections, Explaining (My perfect year would be to sit next to my best friend. My perfect year would be to get a good teacher . . .)

COMPREHENSION PROCESSES

Understand, Apply

PROCEDURES

Introducing Vocabulary

> ☆ perfect ☆ respect
> ☆ inventor ☆ plain ☆ scowl

- For each vocabulary word, have students read the word by parts, then read the whole word.
- Read the student-friendly explanations to students as they follow with their fingers. Then have students use the vocabulary word by following the gray text.
- Review and discuss the photos and illustrations.

USING VOCABULARY

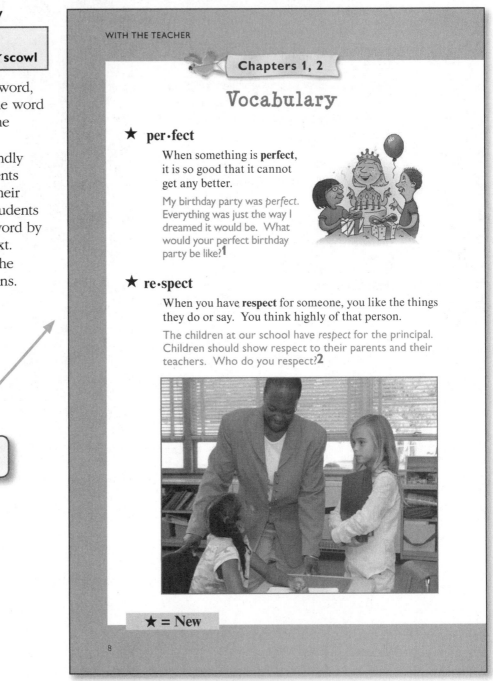

WITH THE TEACHER

Chapters 1, 2

Vocabulary

★ **per·fect**

When something is **perfect**, it is so good that it cannot get any better.

My birthday party was *perfect*. Everything was just the way I dreamed it would be. What would your perfect birthday party be like?**1**

★ **re·spect**

When you have **respect** for someone, you like the things they do or say. You think highly of that person.

The children at our school have *respect* for the principal. Children should show respect to their parents and their teachers. Who do you respect?**2**

★ = New

8

---

1 **Apply:** Making Connections; Using Vocabulary—**perfect** (My perfect birthday party would be a trip to the zoo with my two best friends. We would eat ice cream and visit the monkey cage.)

2 **Apply:** Using Vocabulary—**respect** (I respect my parents and grandparents. I respect my coach . . .)

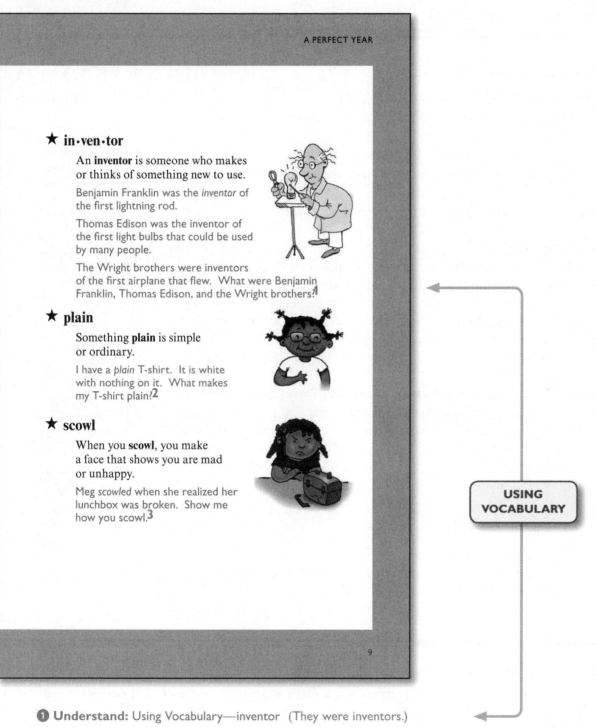

A PERFECT YEAR

★ in·ven·tor

An **inventor** is someone who makes or thinks of something new to use.

Benjamin Franklin was the *inventor* of the first lightning rod.

Thomas Edison was the inventor of the first light bulbs that could be used by many people.

The Wright brothers were inventors of the first airplane that flew. What were Benjamin Franklin, Thomas Edison, and the Wright brothers?[1]

★ plain

Something **plain** is simple or ordinary.

I have a *plain* T-shirt. It is white with nothing on it. What makes my T-shirt plain?[2]

★ scowl

When you **scowl**, you make a face that shows you are mad or unhappy.

Meg *scowled* when she realized her lunchbox was broken. Show me how you scowl.[3]

USING VOCABULARY

9

❶ **Understand:** Using Vocabulary—inventor (They were inventors.)

❷ **Understand:** Defining and Using Vocabulary—plain (It is simple and has nothing on it.)

❸ **Apply:** Demonstrating; Using Vocabulary—scowl

CHAPTER 1 INSTRUCTIONS
Students read Chapter 1 with the teacher.

COMPREHENSION PROCESSES
Remember, Understand, Apply

PROCEDURES

1. Introducing Chapter 1

Identifying—Title; Inferring—Character Traits
Have students identify the title, then ask the gray text questions.
Say something like:
What is this chapter called? (Mighty Maya)
What do you already know about the main character, Maya?
(She is mighty.)
Hmm . . . If Maya is mighty, she must be very sure of herself.

2. First Reading

- Ask questions and discuss the story as indicated by the gray text.
- Mix group and individual turns, independent of your voice.
  Have students work toward a group accuracy goal of 0–3 errors.
  Quietly keep track of errors made by all students in the group.
- After reading the story, practice any difficult words.
  Reread the story if students have not reached the accuracy goal.

3. Second Reading, Short Passage Practice: Developing Prosody

- Demonstrate expressive, fluent reading of the first two paragraphs.
  Read at a rate slightly faster than the students' rate. Say something like:
  In the first two paragraphs, Maya is talking. We know Maya is mighty,
  so she probably has a strong and confident voice. Listen to me read
  with expression.

  "Hi, my name is Maya. I'm seven years old, and I'm in the second grade.
  Second grade was going to be the *perfect* year. I have the *perfect* teacher . . . "

- Guide practice with your voice.
- Provide individual turns while others track with their fingers and whisper read.
  Provide descriptive and positive feedback.
  [Jaelynn], I loved the way you made Maya sound like a real second grader.

- Repeat with one paragraph at a time. Repeat steps with each remaining paragraph.

4. Partner or Whisper Reading: Repeated Reading

 Before beginning independent work, have students finger track and partner or
whisper read.

5. Comprehension and Skill Work
Tell students they will do Comprehension and Skill Activities 1 and 2 after they read
Chapter 1. Guide practice, as needed. (For teacher directions, see pages 28 and 29.)

6. Homework 1: Repeated Reading

CORRECTING DECODING ERRORS
During story reading, gently correct any error, then have students reread the sentence.

COMPREHENSION BUILDING
- Encourage students to answer questions with complete sentences.
- If students have difficulty comprehending, think aloud with them or reread the portion of the story that answers the question. Then repeat the question.

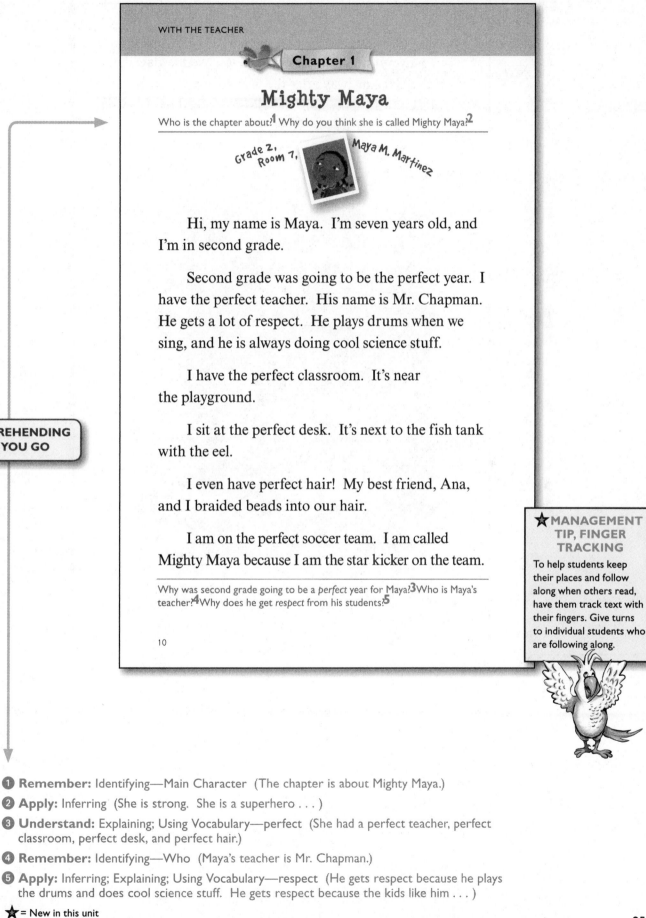

WITH THE TEACHER

Chapter 1

Mighty Maya

Who is the chapter about?¹ Why do you think she is called Mighty Maya?²

Grade 2, Room 7, Maya M. Martinez

Hi, my name is Maya. I'm seven years old, and I'm in second grade.

Second grade was going to be the perfect year. I have the perfect teacher. His name is Mr. Chapman. He gets a lot of respect. He plays drums when we sing, and he is always doing cool science stuff.

I have the perfect classroom. It's near the playground.

I sit at the perfect desk. It's next to the fish tank with the eel.

I even have perfect hair! My best friend, Ana, and I braided beads into our hair.

I am on the perfect soccer team. I am called Mighty Maya because I am the star kicker on the team.

Why was second grade going to be a *perfect* year for Maya?³ Who is Maya's teacher?⁴ Why does he get *respect* from his students?⁵

10

★MANAGEMENT TIP, FINGER TRACKING

To help students keep their places and follow along when others read, have them track text with their fingers. Give turns to individual students who are following along.

COMPREHENDING AS YOU GO

❶ **Remember:** Identifying—Main Character (The chapter is about Mighty Maya.)

❷ **Apply:** Inferring (She is strong. She is a superhero . . .)

❸ **Understand:** Explaining; Using Vocabulary—perfect (She had a perfect teacher, perfect classroom, perfect desk, and perfect hair.)

❹ **Remember:** Identifying—Who (Maya's teacher is Mr. Chapman.)

❺ **Apply:** Inferring; Explaining; Using Vocabulary—respect (He gets respect because he plays the drums and does cool science stuff. He gets respect because the kids like him . . .)

★ = New in this unit

A PERFECT YEAR

Everything was perfect until last Wednesday. It was 10:00 a.m., way after the tardy bell rang, when this kid with spiky hair and glasses walked in. He was no ordinary kid.

What happened at 10:00 a.m.?**1** What do you think the new kid will do?**2**

11

COMPREHENDING AS YOU GO

1 **Remember:** Identifying—Event (A kid with spiky hair and glasses walked in.)

2 **Apply:** Predicting (He will join the class. He will be the new star of the soccer team . . .)

WITH THE TEACHER

Mr. Chapman said, "Class, I would like you to meet Benjamin Franklin Thomas Edison Wright."

I thought to myself, "What kind of name is that? This kid must think he's cool!"

Then things went from bad to worse. Mr. Chapman sat Benjamin Edison Franklin . . . whatever . . . in the chair right next to me! Yuck!

I sighed, "So much for a perfect year."

Why did Maya think that Benjamin Franklin Thomas Edison Wright was no *ordinary* kid? **1** What is Maya's problem? **2**

12

COMPREHENDING AS YOU GO

1 **Understand:** Explaining; Using Vocabulary—ordinary (She thought he was no ordinary kid because he has a long, weird name. She thought that he thinks he's cool.)

2 **Understand:** Explaining—Problem (She has to sit next to the new kid, and she doesn't think she'll like him.)

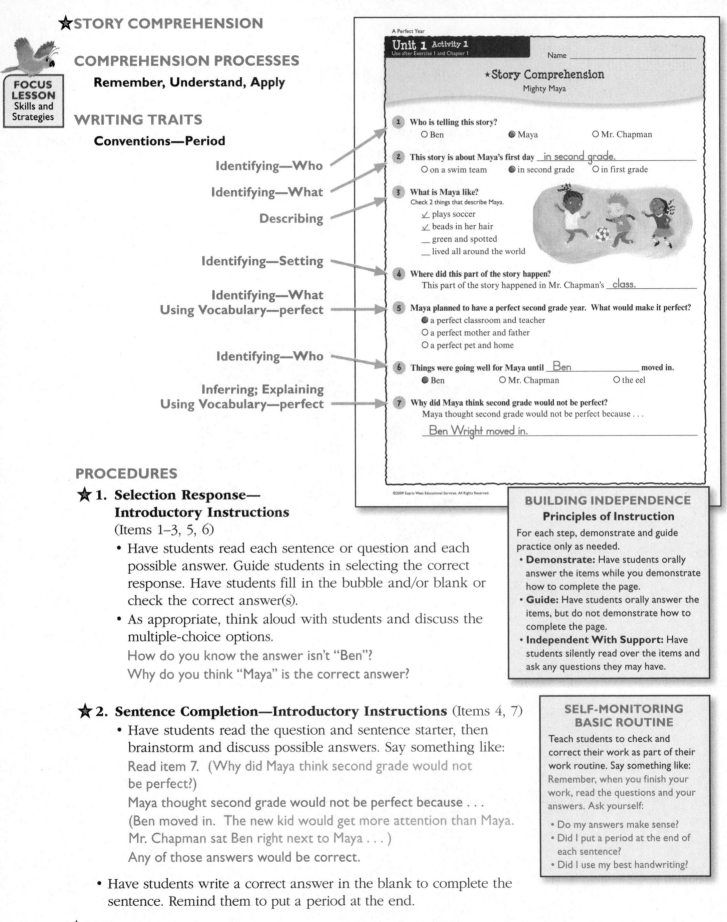

★ **STORY COMPREHENSION**

COMPREHENSION PROCESSES
Remember, Understand, Apply

FOCUS LESSON
Skills and Strategies

WRITING TRAITS
Conventions—Period

Identifying—Who

Identifying—What

Describing

Identifying—Setting

Identifying—What
Using Vocabulary—perfect

Identifying—Who

Inferring; Explaining
Using Vocabulary—perfect

A Perfect Year

Unit 1 Activity 1
Use after Exercise 1 and Chapter 1

Name _____

★ **Story Comprehension**
Mighty Maya

1. Who is telling this story?
   ○ Ben   ● Maya   ○ Mr. Chapman

2. This story is about Maya's first day __in second grade.__
   ○ on a swim team   ● in second grade   ○ in first grade

3. What is Maya like?
   Check 2 things that describe Maya.
   ✓ plays soccer
   ✓ beads in her hair
   __ green and spotted
   __ lived all around the world

4. Where did this part of the story happen?
   This part of the story happened in Mr. Chapman's __class.__

5. Maya planned to have a perfect second grade year. What would make it perfect?
   ● a perfect classroom and teacher
   ○ a perfect mother and father
   ○ a perfect pet and home

6. Things were going well for Maya until __Ben__ moved in.
   ● Ben   ○ Mr. Chapman   ○ the eel

7. Why did Maya think second grade would not be perfect?
   Maya thought second grade would not be perfect because . . .
   __Ben Wright moved in.__

©2009 Sopris West Educational Services. All Rights Reserved.

PROCEDURES

★ 1. **Selection Response—Introductory Instructions**
   (Items 1–3, 5, 6)
   • Have students read each sentence or question and each possible answer. Guide students in selecting the correct response. Have students fill in the bubble and/or blank or check the correct answer(s).
   • As appropriate, think aloud with students and discuss the multiple-choice options.
      How do you know the answer isn't "Ben"?
      Why do you think "Maya" is the correct answer?

★ 2. **Sentence Completion—Introductory Instructions** (Items 4, 7)
   • Have students read the question and sentence starter, then brainstorm and discuss possible answers. Say something like:
      Read item 7. (Why did Maya think second grade would not be perfect?)
      Maya thought second grade would not be perfect because . . .
      (Ben moved in. The new kid would get more attention than Maya. Mr. Chapman sat Ben right next to Maya . . .)
      Any of those answers would be correct.
   • Have students write a correct answer in the blank to complete the sentence. Remind them to put a period at the end.

BUILDING INDEPENDENCE
Principles of Instruction
For each step, demonstrate and guide practice only as needed.
• **Demonstrate:** Have students orally answer the items while you demonstrate how to complete the page.
• **Guide:** Have students orally answer the items, but do not demonstrate how to complete the page.
• **Independent With Support:** Have students silently read over the items and ask any questions they may have.

SELF-MONITORING BASIC ROUTINE
Teach students to check and correct their work as part of their work routine. Say something like:
Remember, when you finish your work, read the questions and your answers. Ask yourself:
• Do my answers make sense?
• Did I put a period at the end of each sentence?
• Did I use my best handwriting?

★ = New in this unit

★MAIN IDEA

COMPREHENSION PROCESSES
Remember, Understand, Apply

WRITING TRAITS
Conventions—Complete Sentence, Capital, Period

Identifying—Who; Viewing

Identifying—What

Inferring—Main Idea

PROCEDURES
For each step, demonstrate and guide practice, as needed. Have students complete the page independently.

★ **1. Main Idea: Selection Response—Introductory Instructions**
(Items 1, 2)
Have students read the question and sentence starter, then fill in the bubble and/or blank with the correct answer. Say something like:
Look at the picture.
Who do you see in the picture? (Maya) What is she doing? (playing soccer)

Now read Item 1. (Who is this picture about?)
Read the possible answers. (Maya, Ben, Mr. Chapman)
Who is this picture about? (Maya) That's right. So fill in the bubble for Maya.

Read the next question. (What is Maya doing?)
Read each of the possible answers. (kicking the ball, feeding the eel, playing baseball)
What is Maya doing? (kicking the ball) Fill in the bubble and write that answer in the blank.

★ **2. Main Idea: Sentence Writing—Introductory Instructions** (Item 3)
- Introduce the main idea sentence. Say something like:
We know who the picture is about. It's about . . . Maya.
We know what she is doing. She is . . . kicking the ball.
Item 3 will help us use that information to write the main idea.
The main idea tells the most important thing Maya is doing. Read Item 3.
(Write the main idea of the picture. Start with *Maya is* . . .)
Let's figure out a sentence that tells the main thing that Maya is doing.
Start with *Maya is* . . . (Maya is kicking the ball.)
That's right. One way to say the main idea of this picture is "Maya is kicking the ball."

- Guide students in writing the sentence, as needed.

> ### SELF-MONITORING
> As a part of your Comprehension and Skill Work routine, have students check and correct their work.
>
> After students complete their work, guide practice as needed.

❶ SOUND REVIEW

❷ ACCURACY AND FLUENCY BUILDING
- For each task, have students say any underlined part, then read the word.
- Set a pace. Then have students read the whole words in each task and column.
- Provide repeated practice, building accuracy first, then fluency.

A1. Mixed Practice
- Set a pace.
  Read each underlined sound and then the whole word.
  Read about this fast: /ŏŏŏ/, Bronx; /āāā/, plain . . .
  Your turn. Start with the first word and keep going.
  (/ŏŏŏ/, Bronx; /āāā/, plain . . .)
- Have students go back and read the whole words.

★ D1. Names
- Tell students these are the names of characters in their story.
- For each name, have students use the sounds they know to figure out the name, then put their thumbs up when they think they know it. Assist, as needed.
  These are names of characters in the story. Look at the first name. Use the sounds you know to sound the word out in your head. Put your thumb up when you think you know the word. **Pause.** What's the word? (Benjamin)
- Repeat to build accuracy, then fluency.

E1. Tricky Words
- For each Tricky Word, have students use the sounds and word parts they know to silently sound out the word. Use the word in a sentence to help with pronunciation. If the word is unfamiliar, tell students the word. Then have students say, spell, and say it.
  Look at the first Tricky Word. It's a compound word. Read the first small word. (any)
  Read the next small word. (where) Read the whole word. (anywhere)
  I lost my bag and couldn't find it . . . *anywhere*. Read the word again. (anywhere)

world	Someday Jillian wants to travel around the . . . *world*.
science	My favorite subject in school is . . . *science*.
scientist	Someone who does experiments in a lab is a . . . *scientist*.
move	Stand very still. Don't . . . *move*.
moved	Eli's family found a new house, so they . . . *moved*.

- Have students go back and read the whole words in the column.

❸ READING BY ANALOGY
- Have students figure out how to say *o-* and *re-* by reading other words they know.
  Read the first word. (no) Next word. (so) Next word. (go) Read the next part. (o-)
  Look at the next two words. Read the underlined part, then the whole word. (o-, over, o-, open)
- Repeat for the next set.

❹ MULTISYLLABIC WORDS
Have students read and finger count the syllables, then read each whole word.

> **TEACHING TO MASTERY**
> **Sounds**
> If you hear an error, demonstrate, guide, and then repeat practice. Say something like:
> Oops, listen. Sometimes <u>a</u> says /ə/ as in ago. Say the sound with me. /ə/
> Have students go back to the beginning of the row and read the sounds again. When students say the sound correctly, say:
> You got the hard sound right!

★ = New in this unit

★⑤ **WORDS IN CONTEXT**

Tell students they can use the sounds they know and then the sentences to figure out how to say each word.

Put your thumb up when you think you know the word. **Pause.** Read the sentence. (I painted a picture.) Say the word. (picture)

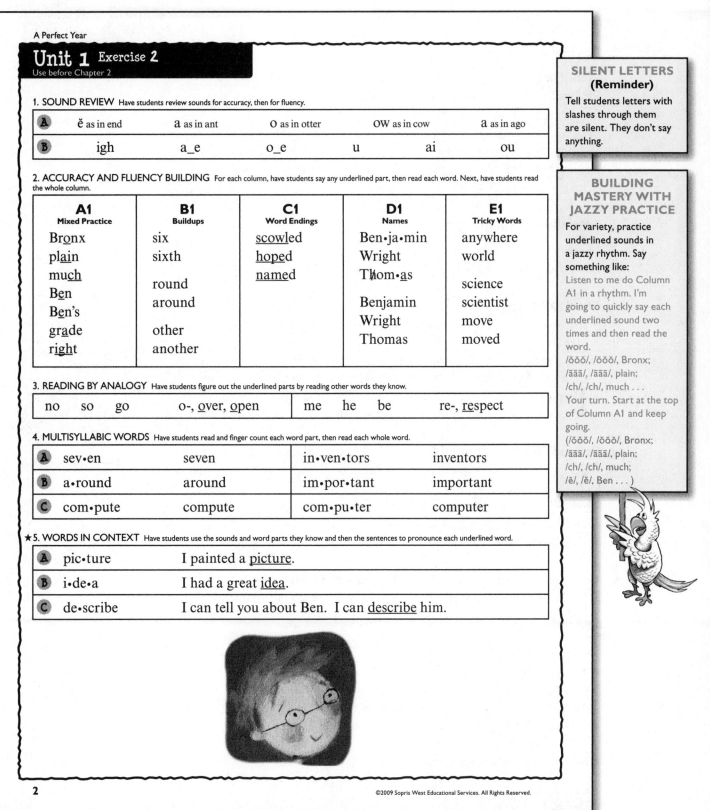

A Perfect Year

Unit 1 Exercise 2
Use before Chapter 2

1. SOUND REVIEW Have students review sounds for accuracy, then for fluency.

Ⓐ	ĕ as in end	a as in ant	O as in otter	OW as in cow	a as in ago
Ⓑ	igh	a_e	o_e	u	ai	ou

2. ACCURACY AND FLUENCY BUILDING For each column, have students say any underlined part, then read each word. Next, have students read the whole column.

A1 Mixed Practice	B1 Buildups	C1 Word Endings	D1 Names	E1 Tricky Words
Bro̲nx	six	scowled	Ben•ja•min	anywhere
pla̲in	sixth	hoped	Wright	world
mu̲ch		named	Tho̸m•a̲s	
Be̲n	round			science
Be̲n's	around		Benjamin	scientist
gra̲de			Wright	move
ri̲ght	other		Thomas	moved
	another			

3. READING BY ANALOGY Have students figure out the underlined parts by reading other words they know.

no so go	o-, o̲ver, o̲pen	me he be	re-, re̲spect

4. MULTISYLLABIC WORDS Have students read and finger count each word part, then read each whole word.

Ⓐ	sev•en	seven	in•ven•tors	inventors
Ⓑ	a•round	around	im•por•tant	important
Ⓒ	com•pute	compute	com•pu•ter	computer

★**5. WORDS IN CONTEXT** Have students use the sounds and word parts they know and then the sentences to pronounce each underlined word.

Ⓐ	pic•ture	I painted a picture.
Ⓑ	i•de•a	I had a great idea.
Ⓒ	de•scribe	I can tell you about Ben. I can describe him.

SILENT LETTERS (Reminder)

Tell students letters with slashes through them are silent. They don't say anything.

BUILDING MASTERY WITH JAZZY PRACTICE

For variety, practice underlined sounds in a jazzy rhythm. Say something like:

Listen to me do Column A1 in a rhythm. I'm going to quickly say each underlined sound two times and then read the word.

/ŏŏ/, /ŏŏ/, Bronx; /āāā/, /āāā/, plain; /ch/, /ch/, much . . .

Your turn. Start at the top of Column A1 and keep going.

(/ŏŏ/, /ŏŏ/, Bronx; /āāā/, /āāā/, plain; /ch/, /ch/, much; /ĕ/, /ĕ/, Ben . . .)

CHAPTER 2 INSTRUCTIONS
Students read Chapter 2 with the teacher.

COMPREHENSION PROCESSES
Remember, Understand, Apply, Analyze

PROCEDURES

1. Reviewing Chapter 1

Identifying—Main Characters; Explaining
Review the main characters and what happened in Chapter 1.
Say something like:
In Chapter 1, you met the main characters. Who are they? (Maya and Ben)
Why did Maya think it was going to be a perfect year? (She had a cool teacher, she had the perfect classroom and desk, she was the star kicker on the soccer team . . .)

2. Introducing Chapter 2

Identifying—Title
Have students identify the title, then ask the gray text questions.

3. First Reading
- Ask questions and discuss the story as indicated by the gray text.
- Mix group and individual turns, independent of your voice.
  Have students work toward a group accuracy goal of 0–2 errors.
  Quietly keep track of errors made by all students in the group.
- After reading the story, practice any difficult words.
  Reread the story if students have not reached the accuracy goal.

FINGER TRACKING

Finger tracking requires each student to pay attention and practice.

4. Second Reading, Timed Reading: Repeated Reading

- As time allows, have students do Timed Readings while others follow along with their fingers.
- Time individuals for 30 seconds and encourage each child to work for a personal best.
- Determine words correct per minute. Record student scores.

5. Partner or Whisper Reading: Repeated Reading

Before beginning independent work, have students finger track and partner or whisper read.

6. Comprehension and Skill Work
Tell students they will do Comprehension and Skill Activities 3 and 4 after they read Chapter 2. Guide practice, as needed. (For teacher directions, see pages 35 and 36.)

7. Homework 2: Repeated Reading

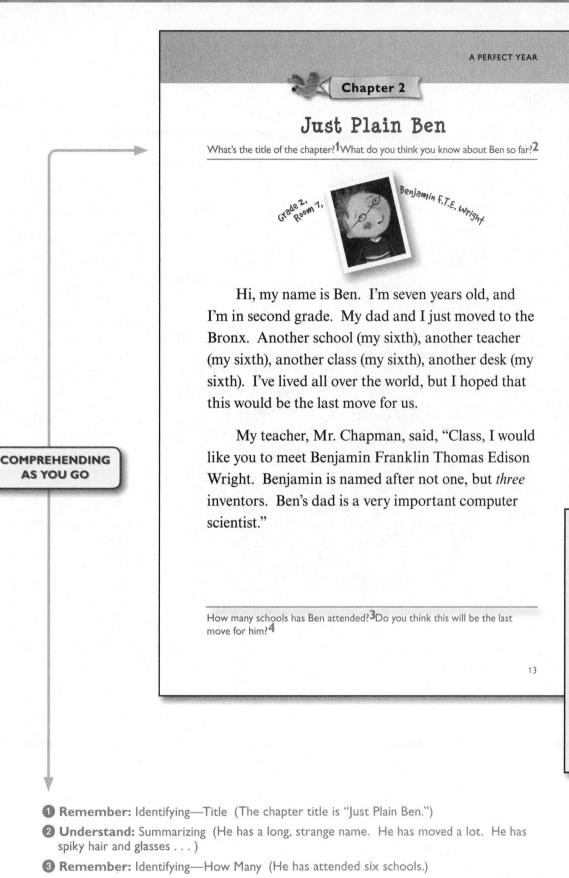

A PERFECT YEAR

Chapter 2

Just Plain Ben

What's the title of the chapter?**1** What do you think you know about Ben so far?**2**

Grade 2, Room 7,   Benjamin F.T.E. Wright

Hi, my name is Ben. I'm seven years old, and I'm in second grade. My dad and I just moved to the Bronx. Another school (my sixth), another teacher (my sixth), another class (my sixth), another desk (my sixth). I've lived all over the world, but I hoped that this would be the last move for us.

My teacher, Mr. Chapman, said, "Class, I would like you to meet Benjamin Franklin Thomas Edison Wright. Benjamin is named after not one, but *three* inventors. Ben's dad is a very important computer scientist."

How many schools has Ben attended?**3** Do you think this will be the last move for him?**4**

13

COMPREHENDING AS YOU GO

FOCUS ON INFERENCE

Identifying—Who; Inferring

After completing the page, say something like:

Who is talking in this chapter? (Ben)

From the book, we learned that Ben has moved a lot. The book doesn't tell us, but since you are close to Ben's age, how do *you* think he might feel about moving so much? (I don't think Ben likes moving. I wouldn't like to move a lot . . .)

❶ **Remember:** Identifying—Title (The chapter title is "Just Plain Ben.")

❷ **Understand:** Summarizing (He has a long, strange name. He has moved a lot. He has spiky hair and glasses . . .)

❸ **Remember:** Identifying—How Many (He has attended six schools.)

❹ **Apply:** Predicting (I think this will be the last move for Ben. I don't think this will be the last move for Ben.)

WITH THE TEACHER

I thought to myself, "So much for the perfect school. I wish I was just plain Ben Wright."

I looked around. The girl with the beads in her hair scowled when Mr. Chapman said that I had lived all around the world. I thought, "I wish I was just plain Ben Wright who had never moved and never lived anywhere but the Bronx."

Then things went from bad to worse. Mr. Chapman sat me right next to the girl with the beads in her hair. Yuck!

Why do you think Ben wished he was just *plain* Ben?**1** What is Ben's problem?**2**

14

FOCUS ON INFERENCE

Reading Between the Lines

Inferring, Drawing Conclusions

After completing the page, say something like: It will be interesting to hear what Ben thinks about his new school.

The book doesn't actually tell us, but we can read between the lines to figure out how Maya feels about Ben. How does she feel about Ben? (She thinks he's ruining her perfect year.)

Why would Maya think that Ben could ruin her perfect year? (She has to sit by him, and she doesn't seem to like him.)

Teacher Think Aloud

I think Maya doesn't like all the attention that Ben is getting.

Teacher Prompt

Do you think she is jealous?

COMPREHENDING AS YOU GO

❶ Apply: Inferring; Explaining; Using Vocabulary—plain (He doesn't like the attention he gets for having a long, strange name and an important father. He wants the other kids to like him . . .)

❷ Understand: Explaining—Problem; Using Vocabulary—scowl (He just moved to a new school. He has to sit next to a girl who scowled at him . . .)

★PASSAGE READING FLUENCY

FLUENCY

Accuracy, Expression, Rate

COMPREHENSION

Understand

PROCEDURES

For each step, demonstrate and guide practice, as needed. Then have students complete the page independently.

★Passage Reading—Introductory Instructions

Using Vocabulary—ordinary

- Have students read the practice words. Say something like:

  Let's practice the words in the bar before we read the story.

  Read the first word. (ordinary)

  When something is ordinary, it's . . . (plain).

  This is a story about something that isn't plain, so it is *not* . . . ordinary.

- Guide practice as students finger track and whisper read the story two times—the first time for accuracy and the second for expression. Say something like:

  You are going to finger track and whisper read the passage—the first time for accuracy. You're going to finger track so you don't skip or misread words. Finger tracking will help you read the words accurately.

  Why will you finger track? (so we can read accurately) That's right. Good readers read the exact words that the author wrote so they can better understand what the author wrote.

  Have students cross out a soccer ball when they finish reading the passage. Repeat the reading for accuracy *and* expression.

- Demonstrate how to do a one-minute Timed Reading. Say something like:

  Watch me do my one-minute timing. If you hear me make a mistake, write a check mark over the word. You can point to each word with your pencil. I'm going to read quickly, with accuracy and expression. After I read the title, I'm going to turn the timer over and finger track as I read. *"No Ordinary Ball.* **Turn the timer over.** I am not an ordinary ball. I am Maya M. Martinez's soccer ball . . . "* One minute is up, so I'll stop and put a slash where I stopped. Then I'll cross out the clock.

  Review errors. Congratulate students on their careful tracking.

- Guide a one-minute Timed Reading. Have students draw a slash to mark where they stop reading after one minute. Have them cross out the timer when they finish.

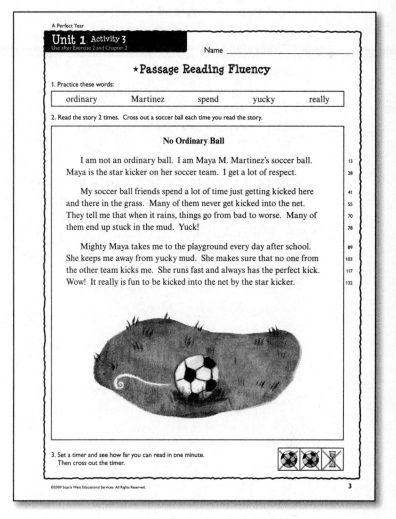

★ = New in this unit

STORY COMPREHENSION

COMPREHENSION PROCESSES
Remember, Understand

WRITING TRAITS
Conventions—Period

PROCEDURES

For each step, demonstrate and guide practice, as needed. Then have students complete the page independently.

Selection Response—Basic Instructions (Items 1–6)

• Have students read each sentence or question and each possible answer. Guide students in selecting the correct response. Have students fill in the bubble and/or blank or check the correct answer(s).

• As appropriate, think aloud with students and discuss the multiple-choice options.
For item 1, say something like:
Read item 1 and the possible answers. (Who is telling . . .)
What's the answer? (Ben)
How do you know the answer is "Ben" and not "Maya" or "Mr. Chapman"?
(The story begins with "Hi, my name is Ben" . . .)

For item 3, say something like:
Let's look at the things we have checked because they describe Ben.
Does Ben have spiky hair and glasses? (yes)
Has he lived all over the world? (yes)
Was he named after three inventors? (yes)
Look at the directions again. What do they say? (Check three things that describe Ben.)
Do we have three check marks? (yes)
As appropriate, have students complete the activity independently. Remind students to put a period at the end of sentences.

Self-monitoring
Have students check and correct their work.

Identifying—
Narrator

Identifying—What

Identifying—
Character Traits
(Characterization)
Using Vocabulary—
inventor

Identifying—What
Using Vocabulary—
plain

Identifying—What

Explaining; Using
Vocabulary—scowl

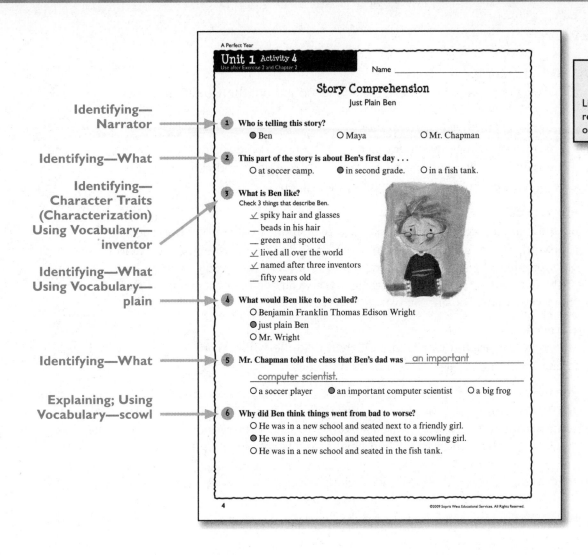

A Perfect Year

Unit 1 Activity 4
Use after Exercise 2 and Chapter 2

Name _____

Story Comprehension
Just Plain Ben

1 **Who is telling this story?**
● Ben   ○ Maya   ○ Mr. Chapman

2 **This part of the story is about Ben's first day . . .**
○ at soccer camp.   ● in second grade.   ○ in a fish tank.

3 **What is Ben like?**
Check 3 things that describe Ben.
✓ spiky hair and glasses
__ beads in his hair
__ green and spotted
✓ lived all over the world
✓ named after three inventors
__ fifty years old

4 **What would Ben like to be called?**
○ Benjamin Franklin Thomas Edison Wright
● just plain Ben
○ Mr. Wright

5 **Mr. Chapman told the class that Ben's dad was** _an important_ _____
computer scientist.
○ a soccer player   ● an important computer scientist   ○ a big frog

6 **Why did Ben think things went from bad to worse?**
○ He was in a new school and seated next to a friendly girl.
● He was in a new school and seated next to a scowling girl.
○ He was in a new school and seated in the fish tank.

4

CHECKOUT OPPORTUNITY

Listen to your students read individually while others work.

① SOUND REVIEW

② SHIFTY WORD BLENDING

For each word, have students say the underlined sound, sound out the word, and say it.

③ ACCURACY AND FLUENCY BUILDING

- For each task, have students say any underlined part, then read the word.
- Set a pace. Then have students read the whole words in each task and column.
- Provide repeated practice, building accuracy first, then fluency.

B1. Compound Words

- Remind students that compound words have two small words in one big word.
- For each word, have students figure out each compound word silently, then read the word. Say something like: These are compound words. They have two small words in each big word. Look at the first word. Figure out the word in your head. Put your thumb up when you think you know the word. **Pause.** What's the word? (doorbell)

C1, D1. Word Endings

- Have students read each underlined part, then read the whole word.
- Repeat practice, building accuracy first, then fluency.

E1. Tricky Words

- For each Tricky Word, have students use the sounds and word parts they know to silently sound out the word. Use the word in a sentence to help with pronunciation. If the word is unfamiliar, tell students the word. Then have students say, spell, and say it.

  Try to sound out the first Tricky Word in your head. Thumbs up when you know the word. Use my sentence to help you pronounce the word. Vicki pushed the wagon, and I . . . *pulled.* Spell the word. (p-u-l-l-e-d) Read the word three times. (pulled, pulled, pulled)

  moved   We pushed and pulled and finally the wagon . . . *moved.*

- Have students go back and read the whole words in the column.

E2. Reading by Analogy

Have students figure out how to say *o-* by reading other words they know.

★④ RHYMING WORDS

Tell students that these words rhyme, or end, with the same sound. Have them read each set of words.

⑤ MULTISYLLABIC WORDS

For each word, have students read each syllable out loud, finger count the syllables, then tell how many syllables are in the word. Have students read the whole word.

computers	3 syllables	Kids like to play games on . . . *computers.*
family	3 syllables	I have four brothers and three sisters. I have a large . . . *family.*
exactly	3 syllables	Another way to say *just right* is . . . *exactly* . . . right.
hesitate	3 syllables	When you pause for a moment, you . . . *hesitate.*
speechless	2 syllables	He couldn't think of anything to say. He was . . . *speechless.*
apartment	3 syllables	I live in a building with many homes. My home is called an . . . *apartment.*
ordinary	4 syllables	My day was the same as always. It was . . . *ordinary.*
shuffled	2 syllables	He walked by dragging his feet across the room. He . . . *shuffled.*

★ = New in this unit

A Perfect Year

Unit 1 Exercise 3
Use before Chapter 3

1. SOUND REVIEW Use selected Sound Cards from Unit 1.

2. SHIFTY WORD BLENDING For each word, have students say the underlined part, sound out smoothly, then read the word.

l<u>a</u>nd	b<u>a</u>nd	b<u>e</u>nd	b<u>o</u>nd	b<u>ou</u>nd

3. ACCURACY AND FLUENCY BUILDING For each column, have students say any underlined part, then read each word. Next, have students read the whole column.

A1 Mixed Practice	B1 Compound Words	C1 Word Endings	D1 Word Endings	E1 Tricky Words
J<u>o</u>nes	doorbell	<u>pout</u>ing	amaze	pulled
m<u>oo</u>dy	downstairs	<u>blurt</u>ed	amazed	moved
m<u>ou</u>th	without	<u>bound</u>ing		**E2** Reading by Analogy
sh<u>ou</u>ted	himself	<u>buzz</u>ed	glare	
h<u>e</u>re	whoever	<u>do</u>ing	glaring	no
pl<u>ea</u>se		<u>stop</u>ping		o-
cou<u>ch</u>		<u>drop</u>ped	spike	<u>o</u>pen
		<u>tug</u>ged	spiky	<u>o</u>ver

★ **4. RHYMING WORDS** Have students read each word set for accuracy, then fluency. Ask how the words are the same.

or	floor	door	way	they	hey	other	another	brother

5. MULTISYLLABIC WORDS Have students read and finger count each word part, then read each whole word.

A	com·pu·ters	computers	fam·i·ly	family
B	ex·act·ly	exactly	hes·i·tate	hesitate
C	speech·less	speechless	a·part·ment	apartment
D	or·di·nar·y	ordinary	shuf·fled	shuffled

3

APPROPRIATE CORRECTIONS

Write any difficult words on a board or clipboard.

Single-Syllable Pattern Words
Have students identify the difficult sound, then sound out and say the word.

Multisyllabic Words
Draw loops under each word part and then guide practice with your hand.

Tricky Words
Have students sound out or read the word by parts, then say the word. Next have students say, spell, and say the word.

After gently correcting a word with the group, go on to other tasks or words. Return to the difficult word at least three times.

TRICKY WORD CORRECTIONS

If you hear an error, write the word on the board. Provide gentle *group* corrections.

- Have students sound out the word to get a close approximation.
  Sound out the word. (/p-ŭ-ŭ-l-l-l-ĕ-ĕ-ĕ-d/)
- Have students use the word in a sentence.
  We pushed and . . . *pulled*.
  Read the word. (pulled)
- Have students spell the word. (p-u-l-l-e-d)
- Return to difficult words throughout the lesson.

COMPREHENSION PROCESSES

Understand, Apply

PROCEDURES

Introducing Vocabulary

> perfect, plain ☆ pout
> ☆ speechless ☆ amazed

- For each vocabulary word, have students read the word by parts, then read the whole word.
- Read the student-friendly explanations to students as they follow with their fingers. Then have students use the vocabulary word by following the gray text.
- Review and discuss the illustrations.

USING VOCABULARY

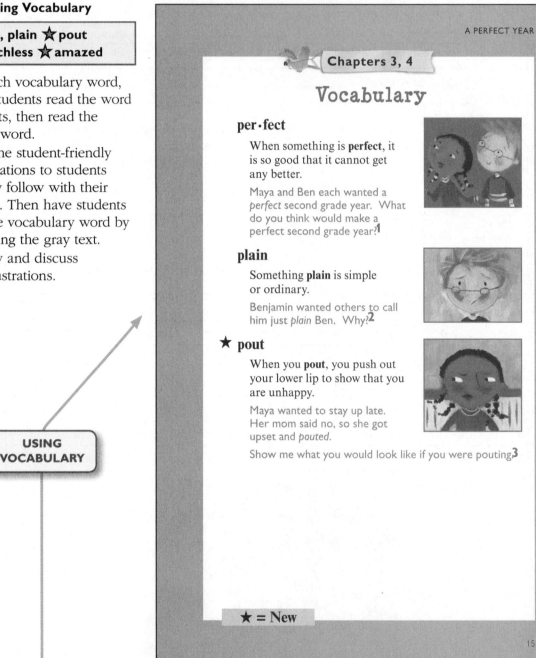

A PERFECT YEAR

Chapters 3, 4

Vocabulary

per·fect

When something is **perfect**, it is so good that it cannot get any better.

Maya and Ben each wanted a *perfect* second grade year. What do you think would make a perfect second grade year?[1]

plain

Something **plain** is simple or ordinary.

Benjamin wanted others to call him just *plain* Ben. Why?[2]

★ pout

When you **pout**, you push out your lower lip to show that you are unhappy.

Maya wanted to stay up late. Her mom said no, so she got upset and *pouted*.

Show me what you would look like if you were pouting.[3]

★ = New

15

❶ **Apply:** Making Connections; Using Vocabulary—perfect (In a perfect second grade year, I would get good math grades, I would make every basketball shot, and I would make lots of new friends . . .)

❷ **Understand:** Using Vocabulary—plain, ordinary (Ben wanted to be more ordinary so he would fit in with the other kids . . .)

❸ **Apply:** Demonstrating; Using Vocabulary—pout

WITH THE TEACHER

★ **speech·less**

If you are so surprised you can't think of what to say, you are **speechless**.

Maya was so surprised to get a bike for her birthday that she was *speechless*. What did she say?**1**

★ **a·mazed**

When you are **amazed**, you are surprised, often in a good way.

I was *amazed* when my friend rode a big horse. Why was I amazed?**2**

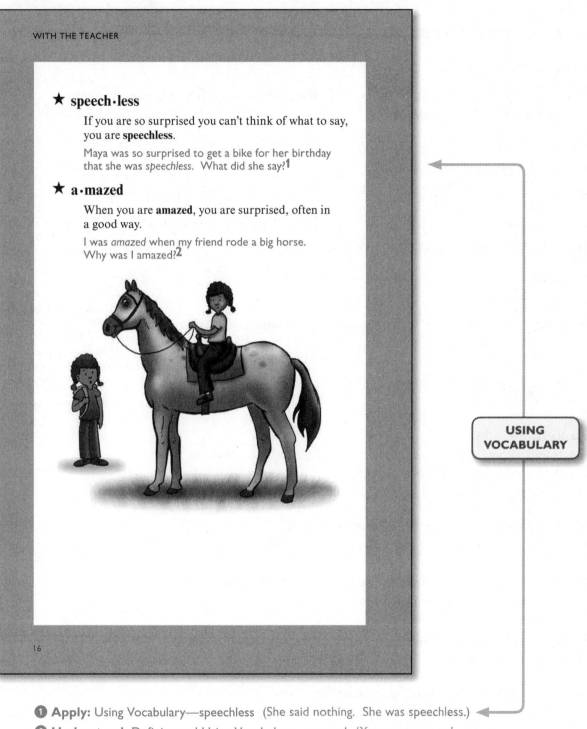

16

USING VOCABULARY

❶ **Apply:** Using Vocabulary—speechless (She said nothing. She was speechless.)

❷ **Understand:** Defining and Using Vocabulary—amazed (You were amazed because you were surprised and happy that your friend could do it . . .)

CHAPTER 3 INSTRUCTIONS
Students read Chapter 3 with the teacher.

COMPREHENSION PROCESSES
Remember, Understand, Apply

PROCEDURES

1. **Reviewing Chapters 1 and 2**

   Identifying—Main Characters, Problem; Describing—Main Characters (Characterization)
   Have students identify the main characters and what happened in Chapters 1 and 2.
   Say something like:
   In Chapters 1 and 2, you met the main characters. Who are they? (Maya and Ben)
   What do you know about Maya?
   (Maya is sure of herself. She likes things to be perfect. She is jealous of Ben . . .)
   What do you know about Ben?
   (Ben has moved a lot. He wants to stay in one place and get less attention.)
   What is Maya's problem? (Maya is upset about Ben. She doesn't like Ben getting all
   the attention.)

2. **Introducing Chapter 3**

   Identifying—Title; Predicting; Using Vocabulary—ordinary
   Discuss the new chapter. Say something like:
   What's the name of this chapter? (No Ordinary Room)
   What do you think this chapter will be about?
   (It will be about a special room. It will be about Maya and Ben's classroom.)

   > **CORRECTING DECODING ERRORS**
   > During story reading, gently correct any error, then have students reread the sentence.

3. **First Reading**
   - Ask questions and discuss the story as indicated by the gray text.
   - Mix group and individual turns, independent of your voice.
     Have students work toward a group accuracy goal of 0–3 errors.
     Quietly keep track of errors made by all students in the group.
   - After reading the story, practice any difficult words.
     Reread the story if students have not reached the accuracy goal.

4. **Second Reading, Short Passage Practice: Developing Prosody**
   - Demonstrate expressive, fluent reading of the first two paragraphs.
   - Guide practice with your voice.
   - Provide individual turns while others track with their fingers and whisper read.
   - Repeat with one paragraph or page at a time.

5. **Partner or Whisper Reading: Repeated Reading**
    Before beginning independent work, have students finger track and partner or
   whisper read.

6. **Comprehension and Skill Work**
   Tell students they will do Comprehension and Skill Activities 5 and 6 after they read
   Chapter 3. Guide practice, as needed. (For teacher directions, see pages 46 and 47.)

7. Homework 3: Repeated Reading

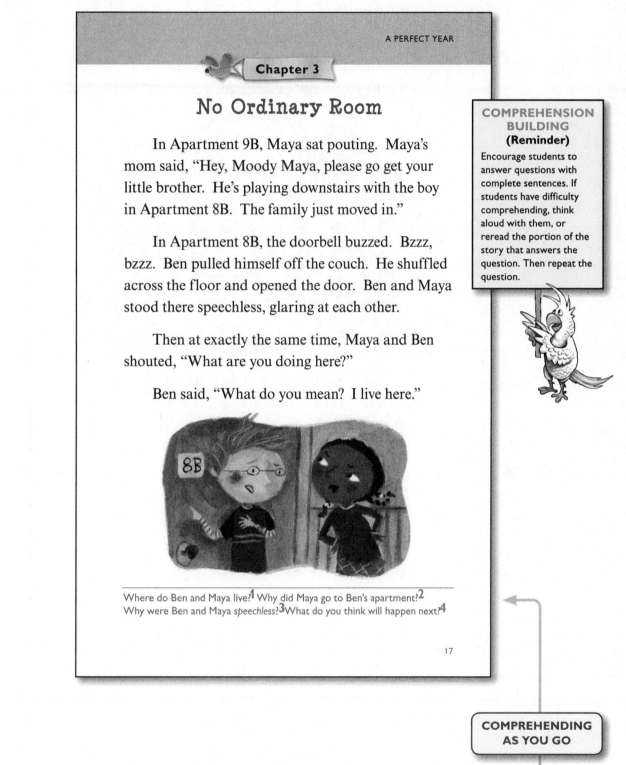

A PERFECT YEAR

Chapter 3

No Ordinary Room

In Apartment 9B, Maya sat pouting. Maya's mom said, "Hey, Moody Maya, please go get your little brother. He's playing downstairs with the boy in Apartment 8B. The family just moved in."

In Apartment 8B, the doorbell buzzed. Bzzz, bzzz. Ben pulled himself off the couch. He shuffled across the floor and opened the door. Ben and Maya stood there speechless, glaring at each other.

Then at exactly the same time, Maya and Ben shouted, "What are you doing here?"

Ben said, "What do you mean? I live here."

Where do Ben and Maya live?**1** Why did Maya go to Ben's apartment?**2**
Why were Ben and Maya *speechless*?**3** What do you think will happen next?**4**

17

COMPREHENSION BUILDING (Reminder)

Encourage students to answer questions with complete sentences. If students have difficulty comprehending, think aloud with them, or reread the portion of the story that answers the question. Then repeat the question.

COMPREHENDING AS YOU GO

❶ **Apply:** Inferring—Where (Ben and Maya live in the same apartment building.)

❷ **Understand:** Explaining (She went to get her little brother.)

❸ **Apply:** Inferring; Using Vocabulary—speechless (They were speechless because they were surprised to see each other.)

❹ **Apply:** Predicting (They will become friends. They will be unhappy that they are neighbors.)

WITH THE TEACHER

Just then Maya's little brother, BJ, came bounding from another room. BJ tugged at Maya, "Come see the computer room!"

Maya hesitated. Then she went with BJ into the other room. Ben's little brother sat at one computer, and a man with big round glasses and spiky hair sat at another computer.

Maya's mouth dropped open. She was amazed. This was no ordinary room. One, two, three, four, five . . . There were five computers in the room!

Where did Maya's little brother take her?**1** Why was Maya *amazed?* **2**

18

COMPREHENDING
AS YOU GO

❶ **Remember:** Identifying—Where (Maya's little brother took her to the computer room.)

❷ **Understand:** Explaining; Using Vocabulary—amazed (Maya was amazed because there were five computers in the room.)

A PERFECT YEAR

Without stopping to think, Maya blurted,
"Wow! Way cool! Way cool, Benjamin, Edison,
Wright, Jones, or whoever you are."

Ben said, "I'm Ben, just plain Ben."

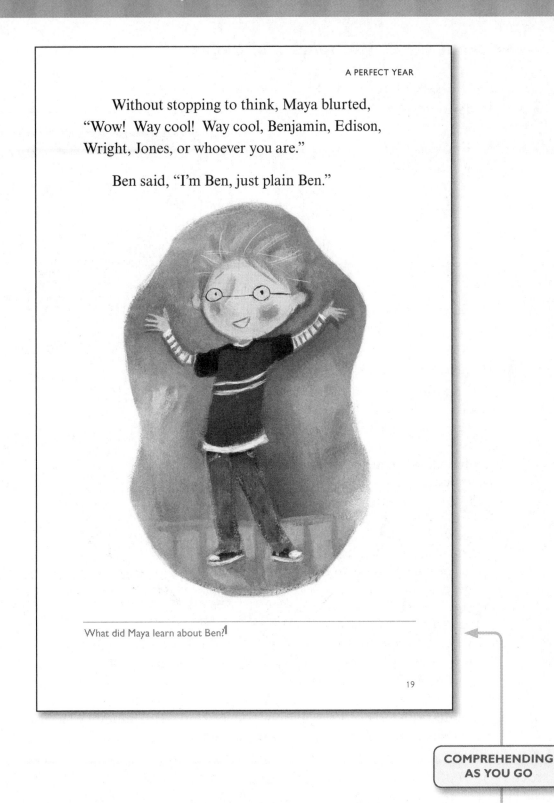

What did Maya learn about Ben?[1]

19

COMPREHENDING
AS YOU GO

❶ Apply: Inferring; **Understand:** Describing—Character Traits (Characterization)
(Maya learned that Ben didn't think he was cool or special. She learned that he wanted to
be called just Ben. She learned that Ben was okay.)

★VOCABULARY AND ALPHABETICAL ORDER

COMPREHENSION PROCESSES

Understand, Apply

WRITING TRAITS

Conventions—Period

Alphabetical Order

**Defining and Using Vocabulary—
inventor
Illustrating**

**Defining and Using Vocabulary—perfect
Illustrating**

**Defining and Using Vocabulary—scowl
Illustrating**

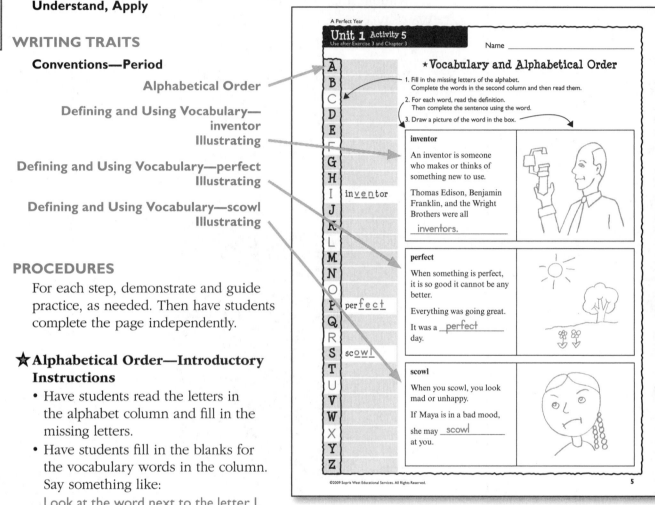

PROCEDURES

For each step, demonstrate and guide practice, as needed. Then have students complete the page independently.

★Alphabetical Order—Introductory Instructions

- Have students read the letters in the alphabet column and fill in the missing letters.
- Have students fill in the blanks for the vocabulary words in the column. Say something like:

Look at the word next to the letter <u>I</u>. The missing word is *inventor*.

It's the same word in the first box. Read the word. (inventor)

Say the word by syllables. (in-ven-tor) What part is missing? (ven)

Write the letters that spell *ven*. Look at the word *inventor* in the box to check and correct.

★Vocabulary: Sentence Completion, Illustrating—Introductory Instructions

- Have students read the vocabulary words and definitions. Say something like:

Read the vocabulary word in the top box again. (inventor)

Now read the definition. (An inventor is someone who makes or thinks of something new to use.)

- Have students read the sentence starters and complete the sentences. Then have them draw a picture of the word.

Now read the sample sentence to yourself, saying *inventors* when you get to the blank.

Everyone, write the word *inventors* in the blank, then draw a picture of the word in the box.

Self-monitoring

Have students check and correct their work.

★ = New in this unit

STORY COMPREHENSION

COMPREHENSION PROCESSES
Remember, Understand

WRITING TRAITS
Conventions—Complete Sentence, Capital, Period, Quotation Marks

Identifying—Main Characters

Identifying—Setting

Inferring; Using Vocabulary—speechless

Identifying—What

Explaining

Identifying—How
Using Vocabulary—pout, amazed

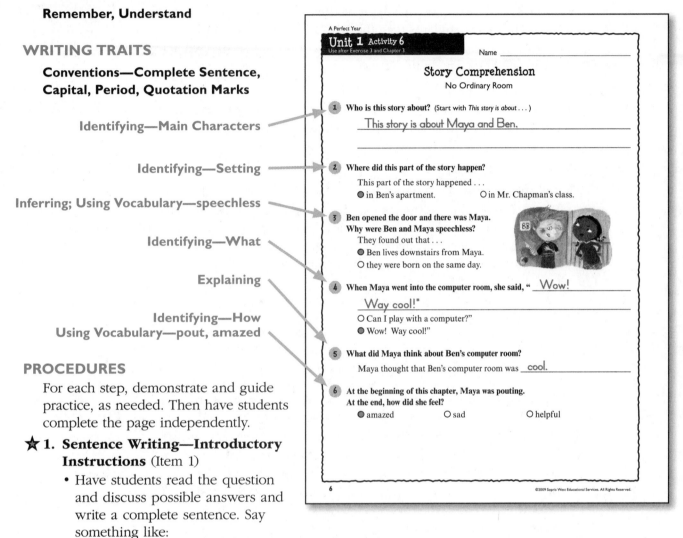

A Perfect Year

Unit 1 Activity 6
Use after Exercise 3 and Chapter 3

Name _____

Story Comprehension
No Ordinary Room

1. **Who is this story about?** (Start with *This story is about . . .*)
   This story is about Maya and Ben.
   _____

2. **Where did this part of the story happen?**
   This part of the story happened . . .
   ● in Ben's apartment.   ○ in Mr. Chapman's class.

3. **Ben opened the door and there was Maya. Why were Ben and Maya speechless?**
   They found out that . . .
   ● Ben lives downstairs from Maya.
   ○ they were born on the same day.

4. **When Maya went into the computer room, she said, "** Wow! Way cool!"
   ○ Can I play with a computer?"
   ● Wow! Way cool!"

5. **What did Maya think about Ben's computer room?**
   Maya thought that Ben's computer room was cool.

6. **At the beginning of this chapter, Maya was pouting. At the end, how did she feel?**
   ● amazed   ○ sad   ○ helpful

6   ©2009 Sopris West Educational Services. All Rights Reserved.

PROCEDURES
For each step, demonstrate and guide practice, as needed. Then have students complete the page independently.

★ **1. Sentence Writing—Introductory Instructions** (Item 1)
   • Have students read the question and discuss possible answers and write a complete sentence. Say something like:

   Read the first question. (Who is this story about?) Who is this story about? (Maya and Ben)

   To answer this question, you're going to write a complete sentence. *Read Well* is full of hints to help you be successful. The directions are in parentheses and will help you write a complete sentence. (Start with *This story is about . . .*) If you start your sentence with "This story is about . . . ," you will end up with a complete sentence.

   Remember to start with a capital letter and end with a period.
   Use your best handwriting, and keep your letters on the lines.

2. Selection Response—Specific Instructions (Items 2–4, 6)
   • Have students read each sentence or question, then fill in the bubble and/or blank with the correct answer. Remind students to put a period at the end of sentences and/or copy the punctuation correctly.
   • For Item 4, show or guide students in copying the ending quotation marks.

3. Sentence Completion—Basic Instructions (Item 5)
   Have students read the question and sentence starter. Have them write an answer that correctly completes the sentence. Remind students to put a period at the end of sentences.

① SOUND REVIEW

PACING
Exercise 4a should take about 10 minutes, allowing about 10 minutes for the Focus Lesson.

② ACCURACY AND FLUENCY BUILDING

- For each task, have students say any underlined part, then read the word.
- Set a pace. Then have students read the whole words in each task and column.
- Provide repeated practice, building accuracy first, then fluency.

B1. Contractions

- Have students read "did not." Tell students the next word is a short way to say "did not." Then have students read the contraction.
- Repeat with: It's, there's, we're.

⭐ D1. Places

- Tell students these are the names of places they will read about in the story.
- For each place, have students use the sounds they know to figure it out, then put their thumbs up when they think they know the word. Assist, as needed. Use each word in a sentence, as needed. Say something like:

    These are the names of different places in our story. Read the first word. (America)
    Miss Tam lives in . . . *America.*

    Look at the next word and complete this sentence: America is also called the . . . *United States.*
    Read the word. (United States)

E1. Tricky Words

- For each Tricky Word, have students use the sounds and word parts they know to silently sound out the word. Use the word in a sentence to help with pronunciation. If the word is unfamiliar, tell students the word. Then have students say, spell, and say it.

    Try to sound out the first Tricky Word in your head. Thumbs up when you know the word. Use my sentence to help you pronounce the word. Sara Jane doesn't live in the country. She lives in a . . . *city.* Spell the word. (c-i-t-y) Read the word three times. (city, city, city)

sorry	Nicholas felt bad that he had lost his dad's book. He was . . . *sorry.*
oh	When Bill said he had a red jacket like mine, I said . . . *"Oh."*
friend	Who is your best . . . *friend?*
Earth	The planet we live on is the . . . *Earth.*
little	The opposite of big is . . . *little.*

- Have students go back and read the whole words in the column.

③ READING BY ANALOGY

Have students figure out how to say *ty-* by reading other words they know.

④ MULTISYLLABIC WORDS

For each word, have students read each syllable out loud, finger count the syllables, then tell how many syllables are in the word. Have students read the whole word.

address	2 syllables	Your street name and number are part of your . . . *address.*
exclaimed	2 syllables	"Well, I'll be!" Miss Tam . . . *exclaimed.*
camera	3 syllables	I like taking pictures with my new . . . *camera.*
appeared	2 syllables	The magician tapped his hat, and a rabbit suddenly . . . *appeared.*

⭐ = New in this unit

A Perfect Year

Unit 1 Exercise 4a
Use before Exercise 4b (Focus Lesson)

1. SOUND REVIEW Have students review sounds for accuracy, then for fluency.

A	-y as in fly	ch as in chicken	ĕ as in end	OO as in moon
B	ow i o	wh	or	sh -ck

2. ACCURACY AND FLUENCY BUILDING For each column, have students say any underlined part, then read each word. Next, have students read the whole column.

A1 Mixed Review	B1 Contractions	C1 Word Endings	D1 Places	E1 Tricky Words
check	did not	<u>turned</u>	America	city
web	didn't	<u>zoomed</u>	United States	sorry
screen		<u>blurted</u>		oh
black	It is	<u>crowded</u>		
North	It's	<u>scratched</u>		friend
whoosh		<u>started</u>		Earth
	there is	<u>buzzed</u>		little
	there's	<u>amazed</u>		
		<u>building</u>		
	we are			
	we're			

3. READING BY ANALOGY Have students figure out the underlined parts by reading other words they know.

by	why	sk<u>y</u>	t<u>y</u>pe	t<u>y</u>ped

4. MULTISYLLABIC WORDS Have students read and finger count each word part, then read each whole word.

A	ad•dress	address	ex•claimed	exclaimed
B	cam•er•a	camera	ap•peared	appeared

4

WORD ORDER • SENTENCE JUMBLE

PREP NOTES
To demonstrate how to comlete the sentence jumble, use an overhead of page 5 in student *Exercise Book 1*, write on a transparency placed over the page, or use a paper copy.

PURPOSE

The purpose of this lesson is to provide explicit instruction in how to sequence groups of words to write sentences that make sense. The lesson prepares students for Comprehension and Skill Work. Students do not write in their books but will watch and respond as you guide them through the lesson.

COMPREHENSION PROCESSES

Understand

PROCEDURES

❶ INTRODUCTION

Explain the purpose of the lesson. Say something like:

Today, we're going to learn how to put words in order so they make sense.

❷ WRITING A SENTENCE THAT MAKES SENSE

Comprehension Monitoring, Sentence Writing

Guide oral responses.

Everyone, look at the first box. Read the words by the first dot. (are perfect)

Those words are part of a sentence, but they don't make sense because we don't know *what* is perfect. Read the words by the next dot. (Maya's braids)

Could the words "Maya's braids" tell us *what* is perfect? (yes)

Our first job is to figure out how we should start our sentence.

If we start with "are perfect," the sentence would read "are perfect . . . Maya's braids."

Does that sound right? (no)

Let's follow the numbers in the parentheses and put the phrases in an order that makes sense. Start with "Maya's braids." Everyone, read with me. Maya's braids are perfect.

Does that make sense? (yes) What's perfect? (Maya's braids)

Repeat with the second and third sentence. Demonstrate how to write each response.

Note: The second sentence can be phrased "My friends play soccer every Saturday" or "Every Saturday, my friends play soccer." Follow the numbers to guide the easiest sequence of words, but acknowledge any correct word sequencing, as appropriate.

❸ GUIDE CHECK AND CORRECT

Guide students in using the Check and Correct procedures.

Find the Check and Correct arrow. Let's use the checklist to see how I did.

Remember, when we finish our Comp and Skill Work, we always check and correct.

Note: After guiding students through the checklist, tell students they should use the Check and Correct procedure when they complete each Comp and Skill activity.

A Perfect Year

Unit 1 Exercise 4b (Focus Lesson)
Use after Exercise 4a and before Chapter 4

FOCUS LESSON Skills and Strategies

Word Order • Sentence Jumble

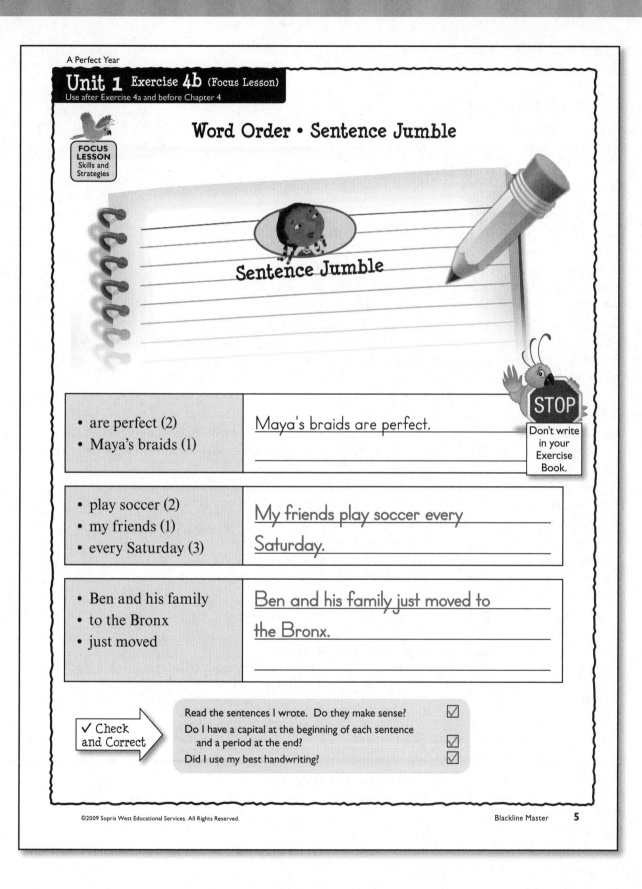

Sentence Jumble

• are perfect (2) • Maya's braids (1)	Maya's braids are perfect.
• play soccer (2) • my friends (1) • every Saturday (3)	My friends play soccer every Saturday.
• Ben and his family • to the Bronx • just moved	Ben and his family just moved to the Bronx.

STOP Don't write in your Exercise Book.

✓ Check and Correct

Read the sentences I wrote. Do they make sense?	☑
Do I have a capital at the beginning of each sentence and a period at the end?	☑
Did I use my best handwriting?	☑

Blackline Master **5**

51

CHAPTER 4 INSTRUCTIONS
Students read Chapter 4 with the teacher.

COMPREHENSION PROCESSES
Understand, Apply

PROCEDURES

1. **Reviewing Chapters 1–3**

   Summarizing—Events
   Have students quickly review the main events from Chapters 1–3. Say something like:
   At the beginning of the story, how did Maya feel about second grade?
   (She thought it would be perfect because she had the perfect class . . .)
   Then what happened? What was Maya's problem?
   (There was a new kid named Ben who got a lot of attention.)
   In the middle of the story, there was an interesting twist. What did Maya find out when she went to get her little brother? (Maya found out that Ben lived in her apartment building. She learned that Ben was just an ordinary kid. She learned that Ben's family had five computers.)

2. **Introducing Chapter 4**
   Have students read the title. Then explain that the Web is a place people connect to on their computers. The Web has a lot of information. Next, have students predict what the chapter will be about by following the gray text.

3. **First Reading**
   * Ask questions and discuss the text as indicated by the gray text.
   * Mix group and individual turns, independent of your voice.
     Have students work toward a group accuracy goal of 0–2 errors.
     Quietly keep track of errors made by all students in the group.
   * After reading the story, practice any difficult words.
     Reread the story if students have not reached the accuracy goal.

4. **Second Reading, Timed Reading: Repeated Reading**

   * As time allows, have students do Timed Readings while others follow along.
   * Time individuals for 30 seconds, and encourage each child to work for a personal best.
   * Count the number of words read correctly in 30 seconds (words read minus errors). Multiply by two to determine words correct per minute. Record student scores.

5. **Partner or Whisper Reading: Repeated Reading**

   Before beginning independent work, have students finger track and partner or whisper read.

6. **Comprehension and Skill Work**
   Tell students they will do Comprehension and Skill Activities 7 and 8 after they read Chapter 4. Guide practice, as needed. (For teacher directions, see pages 56 and 57.)

7. **Homework 4: Repeated Reading**

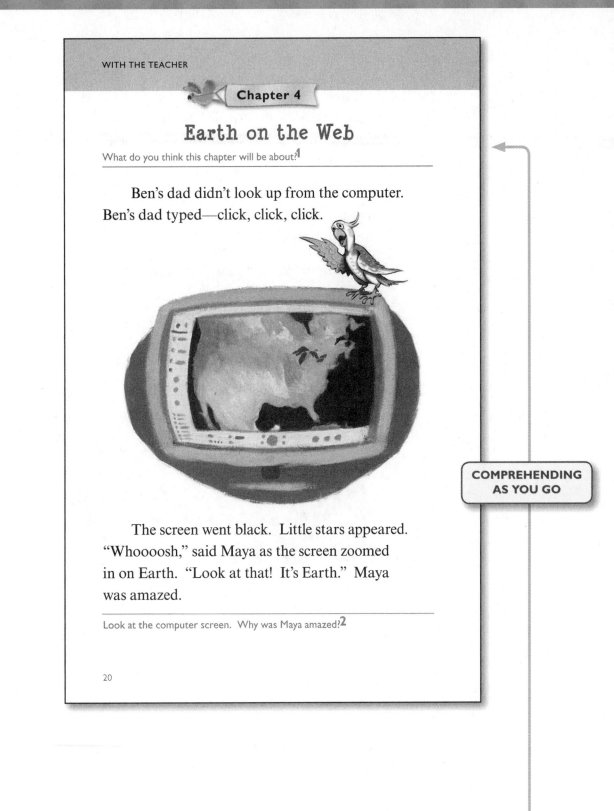

WITH THE TEACHER

Chapter 4

Earth on the Web

What do you think this chapter will be about?[1]

Ben's dad didn't look up from the computer. Ben's dad typed—click, click, click.

The screen went black. Little stars appeared. "Whoooosh," said Maya as the screen zoomed in on Earth. "Look at that! It's Earth." Maya was amazed.

Look at the computer screen. Why was Maya amazed?[2]

20

COMPREHENDING AS YOU GO

❶ **Apply:** Predicting (It will be about the Earth. It will have something to do with computers . . .)

❷ **Apply:** Viewing, Inferring, Explaining; **Understand:** Using Vocabulary—amazed (Maya was amazed to see Earth on the computer . . .)

A PERFECT YEAR

Click, click, click. Ben's dad typed an address. Whoosh! The Earth turned. The camera zoomed in. Maya exclaimed, "It's North America! There's the United States."

"Look, we're zooming in on the city," Maya blurted. "There's the Bronx. Wow! There's our apartment building!"

Ben said, "Wow, it's just like being a bird in the sky. Check that out."

The kids crowded around the computer screen.

Why did Ben say it's like being a bird in the sky?[1] Why did the kids crowd around the computer?[2]

21

COMPREHENDING AS YOU GO

❶ **Apply:** Inferring, Explaining (The picture looks like what a bird would see when it's flying around . . .)

❷ **Apply:** Inferring, Explaining (They wanted to see their apartment building.)

WITH THE TEACHER

Ben said, "We just got back from England. Can we go to England on the computer?"

Ben's dad scratched his head and started to type into the computer when the doorbell buzzed.

"Oh," said Maya. "I bet it's Mom."

Ben and Maya went to the door. Maya's mom asked, "What are you doing?"

Maya said, "Sorry, Mom. This is Ben—my friend Ben—just plain Ben."

What did the kids see on the Internet site?[1] Why did Maya introduce Ben as "just plain Ben"?[2] What do you think Maya and Ben will do in the next chapter?[3]

22

COMPREHENDING AS YOU GO

❶ **Understand:** Explaining (The kids saw North America, the United States, the Bronx, and their apartment building.)

❷ **Apply:** Inferring, Explaining (She knew that's what he liked to be called. She wanted to be nice to him.)

❸ **Apply:** Predicting (They might do more stuff on the computer. They might do a science experiment together . . .)

STORY COMPREHENSION

COMPREHENSION PROCESSES

Remember, Understand, Apply

WRITING TRAITS

Conventions—Period

Identifying—Main Characters

Identifying—Setting

Identifying—What

Identifying—What

Identifying—What
Using Vocabulary—plain

Inferring

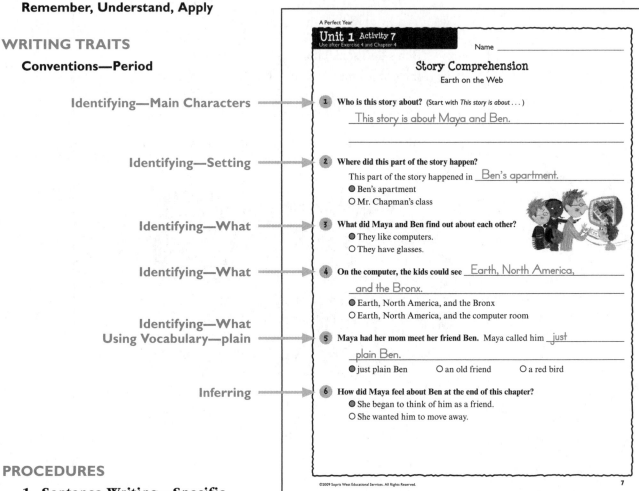

A Perfect Year

Unit 1 Activity 7
Use after Exercise 4 and Chapter 4

Name _____

Story Comprehension
Earth on the Web

1. **Who is this story about?** (Start with *This story is about . . .*)
   This story is about Maya and Ben.
   _____

2. **Where did this part of the story happen?**
   This part of the story happened in Ben's apartment.
   ● Ben's apartment
   ○ Mr. Chapman's class

3. **What did Maya and Ben find out about each other?**
   ● They like computers.
   ○ They have glasses.

4. **On the computer, the kids could see** Earth, North America, and the Bronx.
   ● Earth, North America, and the Bronx
   ○ Earth, North America, and the computer room

5. **Maya had her mom meet her friend Ben.** Maya called him just plain Ben.
   ● just plain Ben   ○ an old friend   ○ a red bird

6. **How did Maya feel about Ben at the end of this chapter?**
   ● She began to think of him as a friend.
   ○ She wanted him to move away.

7

PROCEDURES

1. **Sentence Writing—Specific Instructions** (Item 1)

   Have students read the question and write a complete-sentence answer.

   Remind them to start with a capital and end with a period.

   Read the first question. (Who is this story about?)

   To answer this question, you're going to write a complete sentence. There's a hint to help you write a complete sentence.

   Where is it? (Right after the question, in the parentheses . . .) That's right. Read the directions in the parentheses. (Start with *This story is about . . .*) If you start your sentence with "This story is about . . . ," you will end up with a complete sentence. Remember to start with a capital letter and end with a period. Use your best handwriting and keep your letters on the lines.

2. **Selection Response—Basic Instructions** (Items 2–6)
   - Have students read each sentence or question, then fill in the bubble and/or blank with the correct answer.
   - Think aloud with students and discuss the multiple-choice options, as needed.
   - Remind students to put a period at the end of sentences.

> **SELF-MONITORING BASIC ROUTINE (Reminder)**
>
> Continue teaching students to check and correct their work. Review the Check and Correct procedures by saying something like: Remember, when you finish your work, read the questions and your answers. Ask yourself:
> - Do my answers make sense?
> - Did I put a period at the end of each sentence?
> - Did I use my best handwriting?

PASSAGE READING FLUENCY

FLUENCY

Accuracy, Expression, Rate

PROCEDURES

For each step, demonstrate and guide practice, as needed. Then have students complete the page independently.

Passage Reading—Basic Instructions

- Have students read the practice words.
- Guide practice as students finger track and whisper read the story two times—the first time for accuracy and the second for expression. Say something like:

Remember. You are going to finger track and whisper read the passage. The first time you're going to read for . . . accuracy.

Finger tracking will help you.

Have students cross out a computer when they finish reading the passage. Repeat the reading for accuracy *and* expression.

Now you're going to read for fluency. Remember that means you will read quickly, with accuracy and . . . expression.

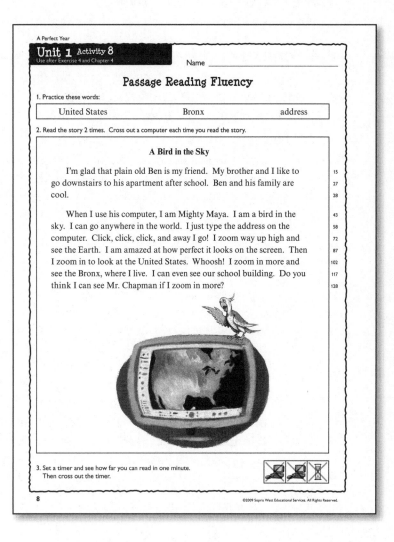

- Demonstrate how to do a one-minute Timed Reading.
- ★You may wish to teach students how to count words per minute. Say something like:

Watch me do my one-minute timing. Finger track and whisper read as I read.

When a minute is up, make a slash mark after the last word I read.

The title is "A Bird in the Sky" . . .

Turn the timer over and read without errors. I'm glad that plain old Ben . . .

What's the last word I read? (building)

Help me count the words. The last complete line I read ends with "and" and the number 102.

So I read 102 words plus. Count the remaining words with me on the next line.

(102 . . . 103, 104, 105 . . . 115) I read 115 words in one minute.

- Have one or two students model the process again, as appropriate.

① SOUND REVIEW

② SHIFTY WORD BLENDING
For each word, have students say the underlined sound, sound out the word, and say it.

③ ACCURACY AND FLUENCY BUILDING
- For each task, have students say any underlined part, then read the word.
- Set a pace. Then have students read the whole words in each task and column.
- Provide repeated practice, building accuracy first, then fluency.

D1. Places
- Tell students these are the names of places in the story.
- Have students use the sounds they know to read each word. Assist, as needed. Use each word in a sentence, as needed.

E1. Tricky Words
- For each Tricky Word, have students use the sounds and word parts they know to silently sound out the word. Use the word in a sentence to help with pronunciation. If the word is unfamiliar, tell students the word. Then have students say, spell, and say it. Try to sound out the first Tricky Word in your head. Thumbs up when you know the word. Use my sentence to help you pronounce the word. Canada is the name of a . . . *country*. Spell the word. (c-o-u-n-t-r-y) Read the word three times. (country, country, country)

banana	My favorite fruit is a . . . *banana*.
through	Instead of walking around the park, we walked . . . *through* . . . it.
learn	We go to school to . . . *learn* . . . new things.
Ana	Our new student's name is . . . *Ana*.
only	Mark thought he had two pencils, but now there's . . . *only* . . . one.
friends	Janice likes to play on the playground with her . . . *friends*.
carry	When Jude goes shopping with his mom, he helps . . . *carry* . . . the bags.
carried	My baby sister couldn't walk, so I . . . *carried* . . . her.

- Have students go back and read the whole words in the column.

④ MULTISYLLABIC WORDS
For each word, have students read each syllable out loud, finger count the syllables, then tell how many syllables are in the word. If needed, use the word in a sentence. Have students read the whole word.

apples	2 syllables	I like to eat fruits such as oranges, pears, and . . . *apples*.
dribble	2 syllables	Todd plays basketball. He can . . . *dribble* . . . the ball.
project	2 syllables	I worked hard on my science . . . *project*.
crayons	2 syllables	Vin colored a picture with . . . *crayons*.
morning	2 syllables	Keisha likes to get up early in the . . . *morning*.
planet	2 syllables	Earth is a . . . *planet*.
Saturday	3 syllables	The first day of the weekend is . . . *Saturday*.
continent	3 syllables	North America is a . . . *continent*.

A Perfect Year

Unit 1 Exercise 5
Use before Chapter 5

1. SOUND REVIEW Use selected Sound Cards from Unit 1.

2. SHIFTY WORD BLENDING For each word, have students say the underlined part, sound out smoothly, then read the word.

ring	rang	hang	hung

3. ACCURACY AND FLUENCY BUILDING For each column, have students say any underlined part, then read each word. Next, have students read the whole column.

A1 Mixed Practice	B1 Bossy E	C1 Word Endings	D1 Places	E1 Tricky Words
now	like	braided	North America	country
beads	spike	teaching	United States	banana
cheese	state	munched	**D2** Compound Words	through
A2 Sound Practice	grade	used	sometimes	learn
away	use		downstairs	Ana
about		spiky		only
along		amazing		friends
amaze				
				carry
				carried

4. MULTISYLLABIC WORDS Have students read and finger count each word part, then read each whole word.

Ⓐ	ap•ples	apples	drib•ble	dribble
Ⓑ	pro•ject	project	cray•ons	crayons
Ⓒ	morn•ing	morning	plan•et	planet
Ⓓ	Sat•ur•day	Saturday	con•ti•nent	continent

> **ENCOURAGING DESIRED BEHAVIORS**
>
> Make a special effort to notice and congratulate the least mature students whenever they are taking steps toward greater cooperation, responsibility, and independence.

COMPREHENSION PROCESSES

Understand, Apply

PROCEDURES

Introducing Vocabulary

inventor, pout, speechless, amazed ★ get carried away

- For each vocabulary word, have students read the word by parts, then read the whole word.
- Read the student-friendly explanations to students as they follow with their fingers. Then have students use the vocabulary word by following the gray text.
- Review and discuss the illustrations.

USING VOCABULARY

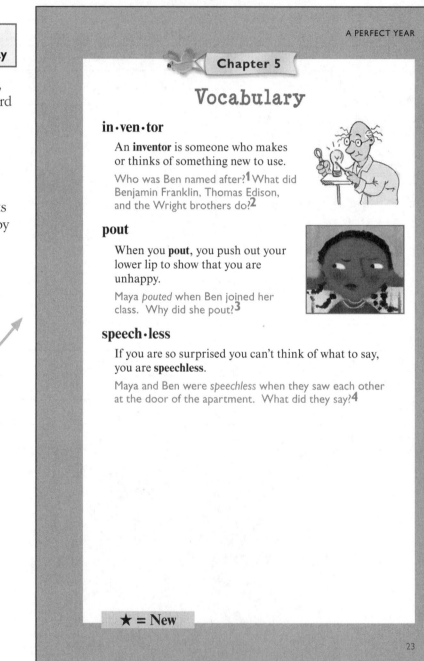

A PERFECT YEAR

Chapter 5

Vocabulary

in·ven·tor

An **inventor** is someone who makes or thinks of something new to use.

Who was Ben named after?[1] What did Benjamin Franklin, Thomas Edison, and the Wright brothers do?[2]

pout

When you **pout**, you push out your lower lip to show that you are unhappy.

Maya *pouted* when Ben joined her class. Why did she pout?[3]

speech·less

If you are so surprised you can't think of what to say, you are **speechless**.

Maya and Ben were *speechless* when they saw each other at the door of the apartment. What did they say?[4]

★ = New

23

❶ **Understand:** Identifying—Who; Using Vocabulary—inventor (Ben was named after three inventors.)

❷ **Understand:** Explaining (They invented things.)

❸ **Apply:** Using Vocabulary—pout (She pouted because she was not happy about the new student.)

❹ **Understand:** Using Vocabulary—speechless (They didn't say anything. They were speechless.)

a·mazed

When you are **amazed**, you are surprised, often in a good way.

Maya was *amazed* by the Internet pictures and maps. What amazed Maya?[1]

Idioms and Expressions

★ get car·ried a·way

If you **get carried away** with something, you do more than you had planned.

Maya and her mom went shopping. They *got carried away* and bought seven bags of groceries. What did Maya and her mom get carried away with?[2] How could you tell they got carried away?[3]

24

USING VOCABULARY

❶ **Understand:** Using Vocabulary—amazed (Maya was amazed by the maps of the Earth showing the United States, the Bronx, and her apartment building.)

❷ **Understand:** Explaining; Using Idioms and Expressions—get carried away (They got carried away with grocery shopping.)

❸ **Apply:** Inferring; Explaining; Using Idioms and Expressions—get carried away (I could tell they got carried away because they bought seven bags of groceries.)

CHAPTER 5 INSTRUCTIONS
Students read Chapter 5 with the teacher.

COMPREHENSION PROCESSES
Remember, Understand, Apply, Analyze

PROCEDURES

1. Introducing Chapter 5

Identifying—Title
Have students read the chapter title and discuss the gray text question.

2. First Reading
- Ask questions and discuss the text as indicated by the gray text.
- Mix group and individual turns, independent of your voice.
  Have students work toward a group accuracy goal of 0–3 errors.
  Quietly keep track of errors made by all students in the group.
- After reading the story, practice any difficult words.
  Repeat if students have not reached the accuracy goal.

3. Second Reading, Short Passage Practice: Developing Prosody
- Demonstrate expressive, fluent reading of the first two paragraphs.
- Guide practice with your voice.
- Provide individual turns while others track with their fingers and whisper read.
- Repeat with one or two paragraphs at a time.

> **CORRECTING DECODING ERRORS**
> During story reading, gently correct any error, then have students reread the sentence.

4. Partner or Whisper Reading: Repeated Reading

 beginning independent work, have students finger track and ~~er~~ or whisper read.

5. Comprehension and Skill Work
Tell students they will do Comprehension and Skill Activities 9 and 10 after they read Chapter 5. Guide practice, as needed. (For teacher directions, see pages 67 and 68.)

6. Homework 5: Repeated Reading

A PERFECT YEAR

Chapter 5

Perfect or What?

Do you think second grade is going to be perfect for Ben and Maya?[1]

It's me, Maya, again. Ben, Ana, and I all hang out together now. Ana and I still have beads braided into our hair. Ben still has spiky hair, and we all get along.

We all play soccer. My mom helped Ben learn how to dribble the ball.

Sometimes we go to Ana's. She has a yard that we can play in.

Sometimes we hang out at Ben's. He's got all the cool computers.

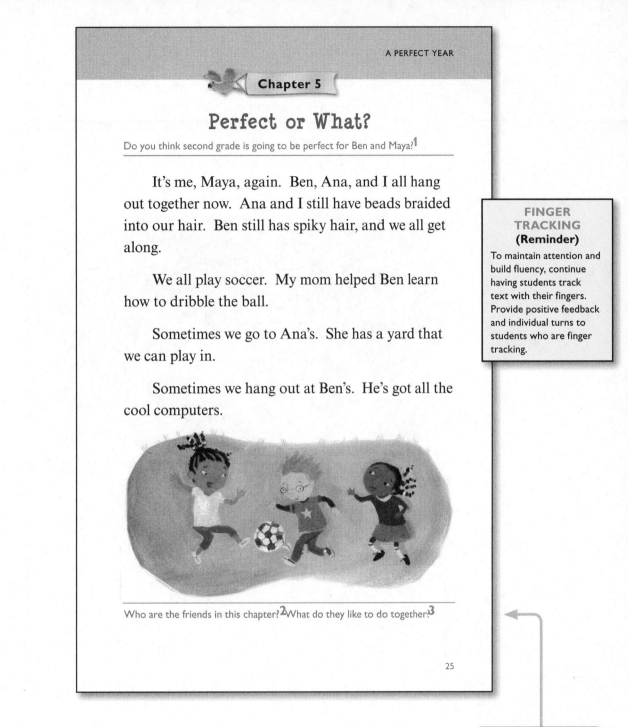

Who are the friends in this chapter?[2] What do they like to do together?[3]

25

> **FINGER TRACKING**
> **(Reminder)**
> To maintain attention and build fluency, continue having students track text with their fingers. Provide positive feedback and individual turns to students who are finger tracking.

COMPREHENDING AS YOU GO

❶ Apply: Predicting (Yes, I think second grade is going to be perfect for Ben and Maya.)

❷ Remember: Identifying—Main Characters (The friends in this chapter are Maya, Ben, and Ana.)

❸ Understand: Summarizing—Action (They play soccer. They play in Ana's yard. They play with Ben's computers.)

WITH THE TEACHER

The three of us like to work on projects together. Mr. Chapman is teaching us about maps.

On Saturday morning, Ana, Ben, and I met to work on a map project. We needed to do only one map, but we got carried away.

Ana, Ben, and Maya *got carried away* with their map project. What do you think they did?[1]

26

COMPREHENDING
AS YOU GO

❶ Apply: Inferring; Defining and Using Idioms and Expressions—get carried away (They did more than they had to. They made a lot of maps. They made cool maps.)

A PERFECT YEAR

By 4:00 p.m., we had munched through a bag of banana chips, three apples, and six cheese sticks. We had used up a box of crayons. We ended up with maps of:

1. Our planet, Earth

2. Our continent, North America

3. Our country, the United States

Amazing! Are we good or what? Perfect project. Perfect snacks. Perfect friends.

Second grade is perfect after all!

What did the kids make maps of?**1** How did Maya's second grade year turn out?**2** How is that different from what she expected when she first met Ben?**3**

27

COMPREHENDING
AS YOU GO

❶ Remember: Identifying—What (They made maps of Earth, North America, and the United States.)

❷ Understand: Explaining; Using Vocabulary—perfect (It turned out to be perfect after all.)

❸ Analyze: Contrasting (When Maya first met Ben, she thought her perfect year was ruined. She didn't like Ben at first, but now they are friends . . .)

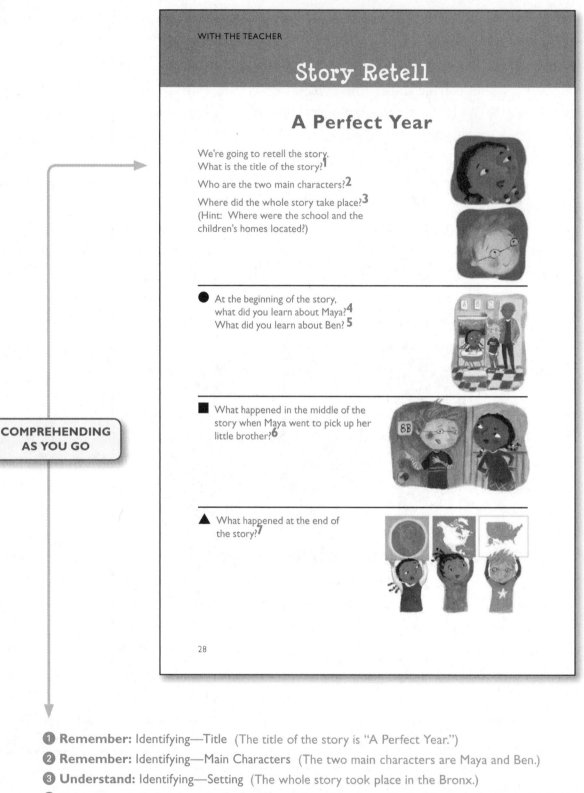

WITH THE TEACHER

Story Retell

A Perfect Year

We're going to retell the story.
What is the title of the story?¹

Who are the two main characters?²

Where did the whole story take place?³
(Hint: Where were the school and the
children's homes located?)

● At the beginning of the story,
what did you learn about Maya?⁴
What did you learn about Ben?⁵

■ What happened in the middle of the
story when Maya went to pick up her
little brother?⁶

▲ What happened at the end of
the story?⁷

28

COMPREHENDING AS YOU GO

❶ **Remember:** Identifying—Title (The title of the story is "A Perfect Year.")

❷ **Remember:** Identifying—Main Characters (The two main characters are Maya and Ben.)

❸ **Understand:** Identifying—Setting (The whole story took place in the Bronx.)

❹ **Understand:** Explaining—Beginning; Describing—Character Traits (Characterization) (Maya is in second
grade. She has beads in her hair. She is the star of her soccer team . . .)

❺ **Understand:** Describing—Character Traits (Characterization) (Ben has glasses and spiky hair. He has lived
in many different places. He has a long, strange name . . .)

❻ **Understand:** Explaining—Middle, Action (Maya found out that Ben lived in the same building she did. Maya
and Ben looked at the Earth on the computer . . .)

❼ **Understand:** Explaining—End/Conclusion (Ben and Maya became friends. Maya, Ben, and Ana made maps
for school . . .)

★STORY MAP

COMPREHENSION PROCESSES

Understand, Apply

WRITING TRAITS

Conventions—Capital, Period

Using Graphic Organizer
Summarizing, Sequencing

Identifying—Setting

Describing—Character Traits
(Characterization)

Explaining—Beginning, Goal

Explaining—Middle, Problem
Action Sequencing—Events

Explaining—End, Outcome/Conclusion

PROCEDURES

Use an overhead BLM copy of the story map to demonstrate and guide practice.

★Story Map: Character Web, Sentence Completion—Introductory Instructions

• Guide students as they complete the story map introduction.
A story map is like a road map. It tells us about a story from the beginning to the end. Our maps begin with the introduction. The introduction usually tells about the setting of the story—where and sometimes when it took place. It also tells about the main character.
Find the diamond and the word *Introduction*. Now look at the gray box.
Touch the words *Setting* and *Where*. Where did the story happen?
(Mr. Chapman's classroom)
So we're going write "Mr. Chapman's classroom" in the box at the top.
Next, let's describe the main character, Maya, using a web.
What does the web say about Maya? (beads in hair)
What else do we know about Maya? (plays soccer, is in second grade . . .)
We can write any of those things on the web. They all describe Maya.

• Guide students as they complete the beginning, middle, and end of the map.
Next, we're going to write what happened at the beginning of the story. Touch the circle and the word *Beginning*. In this story, the beginning told us about Maya's goal. Read the sentence starter under the word *Beginning*. (Maya hoped to have a . . .) What did Maya want? What was her goal?
(to have a perfect year) So let's write "perfect year" in the blank.
Now look at the square and the word *Middle* . . .

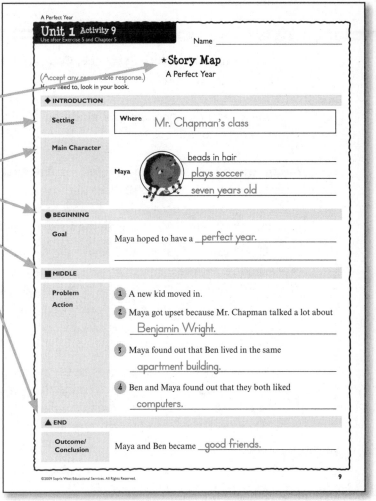

A Perfect Year

Unit 1 Activity 9
Use after Exercise 5 and Chapter 5

Name _____

★Story Map
A Perfect Year

(Accept any reasonable response.)
If you need to, look in your book.

◆ INTRODUCTION

| Setting | Where | Mr. Chapman's class |

Main Character

Maya
beads in hair
plays soccer
seven years old

● BEGINNING

Goal   Maya hoped to have a _perfect year._
_____

■ MIDDLE

Problem
Action

① A new kid moved in.

② Maya got upset because Mr. Chapman talked a lot about
Benjamin Wright.

③ Maya found out that Ben lived in the same
apartment building.

④ Ben and Maya found out that they both liked
computers.

▲ END

Outcome/
Conclusion   Maya and Ben became _good friends._

9

SELF-MONITORING

After completing the Story Map, have students whisper read their answers and Check and Correct. Have students ask themselves:

• Do my answers make sense?
• Did I put a period at the end of each sentence?
• Did I use my best handwriting?

★ = New in this unit

★STORY RETELL • SENTENCE JUMBLE

COMPREHENSION PROCESSES
Understand

WRITING TRAITS
Conventions—Complete Sentence, Capital, Period

PROCEDURES
For each step, demonstrate and guide practice, as needed. Then have students complete the page independently.

★Sequencing Words: Story Retell—Introductory Instructions

- Have students read the phrases and sample sentence in the first box. Say something like:

  In our Focus Lesson, you learned how to put words in an order that makes sense. When we complete this Sentence Jumble, the sentences will retell the story about Maya.

  The first one is done for you. Let's read the first group of phrases, then read the sentence. (would be perfect, Maya thought, second grade)
  Who do you think this sentence is about? (Maya)
  Yes, so the sample sentence begins with "Maya."
  Read the sentence. (Maya thought second grade would be perfect.)
  Does it make sense? (yes)

- Have students read the phrases in the next box, identify who or what the sentence is about, and determine the word sequence.

  Remember, our first job is to read the phrases, then figure out how to start the sentence. Read the phrases in the second box. (came to class, and sat by her, a new kid)

  Who is the sentence about? (a new kid)
  Let's try starting with "A new kid."
  What phrase might come next? Does "A new kid and sat by her came to class" make sense? (no)
  Does "A new kid came to class and sat by her" make sense? (yes)

- Have students write the sentence. Remind them to start with a capital and end with a period.

- Repeat the process with the next three boxes.
- Guide students as they use the Check and Correct checklist.

  Do all your sentences make sense? Do they retell the beginning, middle, and end of the story?

> ### PURPOSE
> **Comprehension Monitoring**
>
> The Sentence Jumble is a simple activity, yet it provides important practice across multiple objectives.
> - Students compose a complete sentence using the scaffold of words provided.
> - Students learn an important self-monitoring strategy. They learn to ask "Does it make sense?" and to fix up work that doesn't.
> - The end product also provides a model of a written retell.

★ = New in this unit

Comprehension Monitoring; Using Vocabulary—perfect

A Perfect Year

Unit 1 Activity 10
Use after Exercise 5 and Chapter 5

Name _____

★Story Retell • Sentence Jumble
A Perfect Year

(Accept any reasonable response.)
Write the words in the correct order to make a sentence.
You're neat, so be neat! Start your sentence with a capital letter and end it with a period. Practice your best handwriting by writing on the lines, leaving a small space between each word, and making each letter the right size.

• would be perfect • Maya thought • second grade	Maya thought second grade would be perfect.
• came to class • and sat by her • a new kid	A new kid came to class and sat by her.
• Maya thought • she wouldn't have • a perfect year	Maya thought she wouldn't have a perfect year.
• had fun with maps • Maya and Ben • on the computer	Maya and Ben had fun with maps on the computer.
• became friends • Maya and Ben	Maya and Ben became friends.

✓ Check and Correct

Read the sentences you wrote. Do they make sense? ☑
Do the sentences tell the story? ☑
Do you have a capital at the beginning of each sentence and a period at the end? ☑
Did you use your best handwriting? ☑

10

① SOUND REVIEW

Have students read the sounds and key words. Work for accuracy, then fluency.

② SHIFTY WORD BLENDING

For each word, have students say the underlined sound, sound out the word, and say it.

③ SOUND PRACTICE

- For each task, have students spell and say the focus sound in the gray bar.
  Next, have students read each underlined sound, the word, then the whole column.
- Repeat with each column, building accuracy first, then fluency.

④ ACCURACY AND FLUENCY BUILDING

- For each task, have students say any underlined part, then read the word.
- Set a pace. Then have students read the whole words in each task and column.
- Provide repeated practice, building accuracy first, then fluency.

★**D1. Story Words**

- Tell students these are words they will read in today's story. Tell them the underlined sounds, then have them read the word.

E1. Tricky Words

- For each Tricky Word, have students use the sounds and word parts they know to silently sound out the word. Use the word in a sentence to help with pronunciation. If the word is unfamiliar, tell students the word. Then have students say, spell, and say it.
  Try to sound out the first Tricky Word in your head. Thumbs up when you know the word. Use my sentence to help you pronounce the word. Katie is a chatterbox. She . . . *talks* a lot. Spell the word. (t-a-l-k-s) Read the word three times. (talks, talks, talks)

another	You can borrow my pencil. I have . . . *another* . . . one.
because	Kirk fell and scraped his knee. He scraped his knee . . . *because* . . . he fell.
every	We always take the bus. We take the bus . . . *every* . . . day.
some	I have lots of pretzels. Would you like . . . *some?*
gives	On Janell's birthday, her family . . . *gives* . . . her presents.

- Have students go back and read the whole words in the column.

⑤ READING BY ANALOGY

Have students figure out how to say *al-* and *re-* by reading other words they know.

⑥ MULTISYLLABIC WORDS

For each word, have students read each syllable out loud, finger count the syllables, then tell how many syllables are in the word. If needed, use the word in a sentence. Have students read the whole word.

forgot	2 syllables	I didn't remember to bring my backpack. I . . . *forgot* . . . it.
feeder	2 syllables	Jim put seeds in their bird . . . *feeder.*
softly	2 syllables	Ella didn't want to wake her sister, so she spoke . . . *softly.*
understands	3 syllables	Speak slowly and clearly so everyone . . . *understands* . . . you.
underline	3 syllables	If you want a word to stand out, you . . . *underline* . . . it.
fiction	2 syllables	A make-believe story is called . . . *fiction.*

★ = New in this unit

Fluency

1. SOUND REVIEW Have students review sounds for accuracy, then for fluency.

Ⓐ	-y as in baby	ea as in eagle	ar as in shark	igh as in flight	a as in ago
Ⓑ	u	ou	er	all	o_e	i_e

2. SHIFTY WORD BLENDING For each word, have students say the underlined part, sound out smoothly, then read the word.

l<u>e</u>d	l<u>ea</u>d	l<u>ou</u>d	cl<u>ou</u>d

3. SOUND PRACTICE In each column, have students spell and say the sound, then say any underlined sound and the word. Next, have students read the whole column.

ai	ow	a_e	igh	ou
ch<u>ai</u>r	n<u>ow</u>	n<u>a</u>m<u>e</u>	s<u>igh</u>	<u>ou</u>t
pl<u>ai</u>n	sc<u>ow</u>l	gr<u>a</u>d<u>e</u>	h<u>igh</u>	p<u>ou</u>t
br<u>ai</u>ded	h<u>ow</u>l	g<u>a</u>v<u>e</u>	fl<u>igh</u>t	sh<u>ou</u>t

4. ACCURACY AND FLUENCY BUILDING For each column, have students say any underlined part, then read each word. Next, have students read the whole column.

A1 Schwa	B1 Buildups	C1 Word Endings	D1 ★ Story Words	E1 Tricky Words
ago	right	slime	p<u>age</u>	talks
amount	fright	slimy	draw	another
along	frighten	starve	<u>c</u>ity	because
about	frightened	starved		every
				some
	car ⤸ care			gives
	scare			
	scared			

5. READING BY ANALOGY Have students figure out the underlined parts by reading other words they know.

all	al-	<u>al</u>ways	<u>al</u>most	he	me	re-	<u>re</u>spect

6. MULTISYLLABIC WORDS Have students read and finger count each word part, then read each whole word.

Ⓐ	for•got	forgot	feed•er	feeder
Ⓑ	soft•ly	softly	un•der•stands	understands
Ⓒ	un•der•line	underline	fic•tion	fiction

ENTHUSIASM

Make a special effort to acknowledge what students can do.

Say things like:
You can read multisyllabic words without help from adults.

You can figure out words you've never seen before.

You can read and use snazzy words like: *another, understands,* and *ordinary . . .* That is very impressive.

7

FLUENCY PASSAGE INSTRUCTIONS

This Story Reading targets fluency as the primary goal of instruction and practice. Students do repeated readings of this short passage to improve accuracy, expression, and rate.

PROCEDURES

1. **Warm-Up: Partner or Whisper Reading**

   Before beginning group Story Reading, have students finger track and partner or whisper read the selection.

2. **First Reading**

   - Mix group and individual turns, independent of your voice. Have students work toward a group accuracy goal of 0–2 errors. Quietly keep track of errors made by all students in the group.
   - After reading the story, practice any difficult words. Reread the story if students have not reached the accuracy goal.

3. **Second Reading, Short Passage Practice: Developing Prosody**

   - Demonstrate reading the first paragraph with expression and fluency. Have students finger track as you read.
   - Have students choral read the first paragraph. Encourage reading with expression and fluency.
   - Repeat with second paragraph.

4. **Third Reading, Timed Readings: Repeated Reading**

    • Select a page. Encourage each child to work for a personal best. Have students whisper read for a one-minute Timed Reading. Tell students to go back to the top of the page and keep reading until the minute is up.
   - Have students put their finger on the last word they read and count the number of words read correctly in one minute.
   - Have students do a second Timed Reading of the same page.
   - Have students try to beat their last score.
   - Celebrate improvements.

5. **Comprehension and Skill Work**

   Tell students they will do Comprehension and Skill Activities 11 and 12 after they read "Eel in the Fish Tank." Guide practice, as needed. (For teacher directions, see pages 74 and 75.)

6. **Homework 6: Repeated Reading**

WITH THE TEACHER

Fluency

Eel in the Fish Tank

by Paula Rich

My name is Eel. I live in the fish tank in 11
Mr. Chapman's second grade classroom. Every 17
school day, a girl with beads in her hair sits at 28
the desk next to me. She's cool. She talks to 38
me softly. She never taps on the glass, and she 48
scowls at kids who do. Best of all, she feeds me. 59

I'm glad she's the eel feeder. I hope she 68
gets to keep her job all year. Last year, I almost 79
starved because the eel feeder forgot. Then 86
another eel feeder gave me too much food, and 95
I got sick. The girl with beads in her hair gives 106
me just the right amount. 111

Some of the kids are frightened of me. I'm 120
big and slimy, and I have lots of sharp teeth. I 131
open and close my mouth all the time, but that's 141
just the way I breathe. The girl with beads in 151
her hair understands me. She's not scared. She 159
gives me respect. 162

Who is telling the story? Who is the girl with the beads? Why does Eel like her?

29

FINGER TRACKING

Reminder

To maintain attention and build fluency, continue having students track text with their fingers. Provide positive feedback and individual turns to students who are finger tracking.

★ TABLE OF CONTENTS AND FOLLOWING DIRECTIONS

COMPREHENSION PROCESSES

Understand

WRITING TRAITS

Conventions—Capital, Period

Following Directions

Following Directions

Following Directions

Using Table of Contents; Identifying—What

Using Table of Contents; Identifying—What

PROCEDURES

For each step, demonstrate and guide practice, as needed. Then have students complete the page independently.

★ 1. Following Directions—Introductory Instructions
(Items 1–3)

- Have students read Item 1, then look on their activity page. Demonstrate an incorrect response. Have students identify what you've done wrong and how to fix it. Say something like:

  This is a fun little activity to see if you can carefully follow the directions.

  Read Item 1. (Underline "Maya and Ben.")

  The Table of Contents is reprinted on your activity from your storybook.

  I'm going to find the words *Maya and Ben* and underline them.

  Ah, *Maya and Ben* is the Unit 1 title. **Draw a line through the title.**

  Put your thumbs up if I followed the directions and thumbs down if I goofed.

  What did I do wrong? (You were supposed to *underline* "Maya and Ben.")

  Oh, that's right. Read the directions for Item 1 again. (Underline "Maya and Ben.")

  I can fix that. **Erase the line through "Maya and Ben" and underline the words.**

- Have students complete the page.

★ 2. Using Table of Contents: Selection Response—Basic Instructions (Items 4, 5)
Have students read the sentences or questions, then fill in the bubble with the correct answer.

Fluency

Unit 1 Activity 11
Use after Exercise 6 and Eel in the Fish Tank

Name _____

★ Table of Contents and Following Directions

TABLE OF CONTENTS
UNIT 1 · **Maya and Ben**

A Perfect Year 7
FICTION · REALISTIC NARRATIVE
With the Teacher
Vocabulary: Chapters 1, 2 8
Chapter 1, Mighty Maya 10
With the Teacher
Chapter 2, Just Plain Ben 13
With the Teacher
Vocabulary: Chapters 3, 4 15
Chapter 3, No Ordinary Room 17
With the Teacher
Chapter 4, Earth on the Web 20
With the Teacher
Vocabulary: Chapter 5 23
Chapter 5, Perfect or What? 25
STORY RETELL 28

Glossary
FICTION · IMAGINATIVE
With the Teacher
Eel in the Fish Tank 29

1 Underline "Maya and Ben."

2 Underline "Chapter 1, Mighty Maya."

3 Draw an X on the word "Fiction."

4 What page does "A Perfect Year" start on?
  ● 7   ○ 8   ○ 10

5 "No Ordinary Room" is the title of …
  ● Chapter 3.
  ○ Chapter 1.
  ○ Chapter 2.

11

★ = New in this unit

MAIN IDEA

COMPREHENSION PROCESSES

Apply

WRITING TRAITS

Conventions—Complete Sentence, Capital, Period

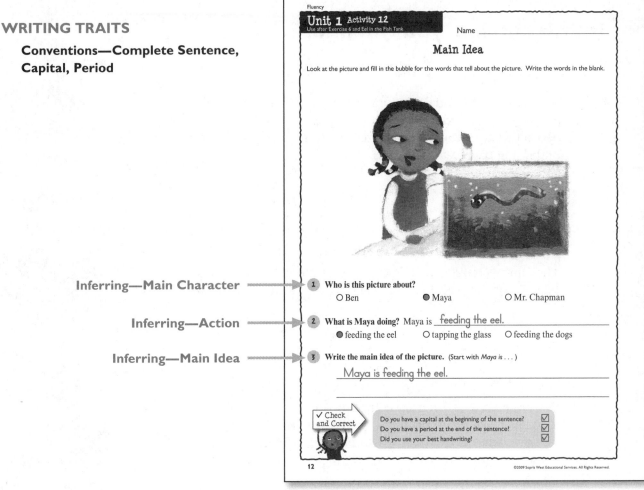

Inferring—Main Character

Inferring—Action

Inferring—Main Idea

PROCEDURES

For each step, demonstrate and guide practice, as needed. Then have students complete the page independently.

1. **Main Idea: Selection Response, Sentence Completion—Basic Instructions**
   (Items 1, 2)
   Have students read the question and sentence starter, then fill in the bubble and/or blank with the correct answer.

2. **Main Idea: Sentence Writing—Basic Instructions** (Item 3)
   Have students write the main idea sentence. Give them the starting phrase and remind them to use a capital and a period.

Self-monitoring

Have students check and correct their work.

End of the Unit

In this section, you will find:

Making Decisions

As you near the end of the unit, plan to give the Oral Reading Fluency Assessment to each child in your group. Use this section as a general guide for making instructional decisions and doing diagnostic planning.

Oral Reading Fluency Assessment

The Unit 1 Oral Reading Fluency Assessment is located on page 79 of this teacher's guide and in the *Assessment Manual*.

Certificate of Achievement and Goal Setting

Celebrate your children's accomplishments. When your students master the unit skills, send home the Certificate of Achievement. Have students set goals for the next unit.

Extra Practice Lessons

Use the Extra Practice lessons for students who need additional decoding and fluency work. Student materials can be copied from the Extra Practice blackline masters.

Making Decisions

USING THE ORAL READING FLUENCY RESULTS

At the end of each unit, you will need to make decisions regarding student progress. Should students go forward in the program? Does the group need Extra Practice before proceeding? Do individuals require more assistance and practice to continue working in their group? These decisions all require use of the oral reading fluency data and professional judgment. As you analyze assessment results, watch for trends and anomalies.

See the *Assessment Manual* for detailed information and instructional recommendations. General guidelines and recommendations follow:

Strong Pass ≥ 101 WCPM 0–2 errors	• Continue with the current pace of instruction. • Have students set goals. (Until students are reading approximately 180 words correct per minute, oral reading fluency continues to be an instructional goal.)
Pass 80–100 WCPM 0–2 errors	• Continue with the current pace of instruction. Consider increasing fluency practice.
No Pass ≤ 79 WCPM **RED FLAG** A No Pass is a red flag. A mild early intervention can prevent an intense and time-consuming intervention in the future.	• If a child scores a No Pass but has previously passed all assessments, you may wish to advance the student to the next unit, then carefully monitor the student. • If a child scores a No Pass but has previously passed all assessments, you may wish to advance the student to the next unit and also provide additional practice opportunities. (See below.) • If a child scores two consecutive No Passes or periodic No Passes, additional practice must be provided. (See below.) • If a child scores three consecutive No Passes, the student should be placed in a lower-performing group.

Added Practice Options for Groups

Warm-Ups: Begin each story reading with a review of the previous day's story. After reading the story, include Short Passage Practice on a daily basis.

Extended Units: If several children begin to score No Passes or barely pass, consider extending the unit by adding Extra Practice Lessons 1, 2, and/or 3. Extra Practice lessons include Decoding Practice, Passage Fluency, and a Comprehension and Skill Activity. (See pages 82 to 92 in this guide.)

Vowel Review: Consider a review of selected vowel units from *Read Well 1* or *Fluency Foundations*.

Added Practice Options for Individual Students

Tutorials: Set up five-minute tutorials on a daily basis with an assistant, trained volunteer, or cross-age tutor. Have the tutor provide Short Passage Practice and Timed Readings or Extra Practice lessons.

Double Dose: Find ways to provide a double dose of *Read Well* instruction:
- Have the student work in his or her group *and* a lower-performing group.
- Have an instructional assistant, older student, or parent volunteer preview or review lessons.
- Have an instructional assistant provide instruction with Extra Practice lessons.

END-OF-THE-UNIT CELEBRATION

When students pass the Oral Reading Fluency Assessment, celebrate with the Certificate of Achievement on page 80.

Note: Using the Flesch-Kincaid Grade Level readability formula, the Unit 1 Assessment has a 2.0 readability level. Readabilities are based on number of words per sentence and number of syllables per word. Adding one or two multisyllabic words can increase readability by a month or two. Though we are attending to readability for the assessments, the overriding factor is decodability.

GOAL SETTING • OPTIONAL

Goal setting is a powerful tool to help children be active participants in the learning process. You may choose to have students do goal setting on a regular basis or periodically to boost motivation. As students complete their Oral Reading Fluency Assessment, you may wish to say something like: [Samantha], you read very well! Let's fill out a goal-setting form. It will tell what you are proud of doing in Unit 1 and what you hope to accomplish in Unit 2.

I'm proud of you because you completed all of your homework for Unit 1. What are some things you are proud of? (learning all the Tricky Words . . .)

Let's figure out what to write on your goal-setting form. It says "I am proud because I can . . . " What would you like me to write? (I am proud because I read all my homework and I can read all Tricky Words really well.) **Complete the first line of the goal-setting form for the student.**

The next line says, "My fluency was _____." How many words per minute did you read? (83) Great, so your goal for Unit 2 is 84. **Fill in the numbers for the student.**

Follow my finger and read the next part of the form.
(To reach my goal, I will: do my best in reading group, read and reread my stories, read my homework.)
I think you will meet your goal of 84! We'll work together. Maybe you can even beat your goal in Unit 2.

Have students sign the goal-setting form to formalize the goal-setting process.

TRICKY WORD and FOCUS SKILL WARM-UP

| again | world | because | wouldn't | thought | yours |

ORAL READING FLUENCY PASSAGE

Maya and Ben

★Hi! My name is Maya. I am in second grade, and this   12
year is great. I live in a cool building, and I have two best friends.   27
My mother, my brother, and I live in the perfect apartment.   38
Today, we are going to braid my hair. Life is good.   49

Hi! My name is Ben. When I first started school here, I   61
thought I might not like it. It seemed like everyone was scowling   73
at me. Now I have a lot of friends. We hang out together.   86
Today, Mr. Chapman said that he would begin teaching us about   97
inventors. I'm named after three important inventors, so that   106
should be fun.   109

We think second grade is going to be perfect. We'll play   120
soccer, work on computers, and have a lot of fun.   130

ORAL READING FLUENCY	Start timing at the ★. Mark errors. Make a single slash in the text (/) at 60 seconds. If the student completes the passage in less than 60 seconds, have the student go back to the ★ and continue reading. Make a double slash (//) in the text at 60 seconds.
WCPM	Determine words correct per minute by subtracting errors from words read in 60 seconds.
STRONG PASS	The student scores no more than 2 errors on the first pass through the passage and reads a minimum of 101 or more words correct per minute. Proceed to Unit 2.
PASS	The student scores no more than 2 errors on the first pass through the passage and reads 80 to 100 words correct per minute. Proceed to Unit 2.
NO PASS	The student scores 3 or more errors on the first pass through the passage and/or reads 79 or fewer words correct per minute. Provide added fluency practice with *RW2* Unit 1 Extra Practice. (Lessons follow the certificate at the end of the teacher's guide.) After completing the Extra Practice, retest the student.

It's No Ordinary Day!

_____

has successfully completed

Read Well 2 Unit 1 • Maya and Ben

with _____ words correct per minute.

Teacher Signature _____

Date _____

✂ -

It's No Ordinary Day!

_____

has successfully completed

Read Well 2 Unit 1 • Maya and Ben

with _____ words correct per minute.

Teacher Signature _____

Date _____

Goal Setting

I am proud because I _____

_____

In this unit, my fluency was _____. My goal is to read _____ (one word per minute faster).

To reach my goal, I will:

- Do my best in reading group

- Read and reread my stories

- Read my homework

Signed _____   Date _____

✂ --

Goal Setting

I am proud because I _____

_____

In this unit, my fluency was _____. My goal is to read _____ (one word per minute faster).

To reach my goal, I will:

- Do my best in reading group

- Read and reread my stories

- Read my homework

Signed _____   Date _____

PROCEDURES

1. Sound Review

Use selected Sound Cards from Unit 1.

- Have students say each sound, building accuracy first, then fluency.
- Mix group and individual turns, independent of your voice.

2. Sounding Out Smoothly

- For each word, have students say the underlined part, sound out the word smoothly, then read the whole word. (Use the words in sentences, as needed.)
- Have students read all the words in the row, building accuracy first, then fluency.
- Repeat practice. Mix group and individual turns, independent of your voice.

3. Accuracy and Fluency Building

- For each task, have students say any underlined part, then read each word.
- Set a pace. Then have students read the whole words in each task and column.
- Provide repeated practice, building accuracy first, then fluency.

4. Tricky Words

Have students read each row for accuracy, then fluency.

5. Multisyllabic Words

For each word, have students read each syllable out loud, finger count the syllables, then tell how many syllables are in the word. If needed, use the word in a sentence. Have students read the whole word.

6. Dictation

cow, scowl, scowling, came, name, same

- Say "cow." Have students say the word. Guide students as they finger count and say the sounds. Have students touch or write the sounds, then read the word. Say something like:

The first word is **cow.** Say the word. (cow)

Say and count the sounds in **cow** with me.

Hold up one finger for each sound. /k/•/ow/ How many sounds? (two)

What's the first sound? (/k/) Touch under /k/.

What's the last sound? (/ow/) What letter pattern makes the /ow/ sound? (o-w)

Write /ow/. Read the word. (cow)

- Repeat with "scowl" and "scowling."
- Continue with the rhyming words: came, name, same.

Unit 1 Decoding Practice

Name _____

1. SOUND REVIEW Use selected Sound Cards from Unit 1.

2. SOUNDING OUT SMOOTHLY Have students say the underlined part, sound out and read each word, then read the row.

m<u>igh</u>t	Br<u>o</u>nx	<u>N</u>orth	br<u>ai</u>d

3. ACCURACY/FLUENCY BUILDING Have students say any underlined part, then read each word. Next, have students read the column.

A1 Sound Practice	**B1** Word Endings	**C1** Rhyming Words	**D1** Buildups
<u>a</u>bout	go<u>ing</u>	other	<u>port</u>
<u>a</u>round	start<u>ed</u>	br<u>other</u>	im<u>port</u>
<u>A</u>merica	turn<u>ed</u>	m<u>other</u>	im<u>port</u>ant
A2 Contractions	seem<u>ed</u>	**C2** Bossy E	<u>part</u>
I'm	zoom<u>ed</u>	n<u>a</u>me	a<u>part</u>
he's	look<u>ed</u>	g<u>a</u>me	a<u>part</u>ment
she's	ask<u>ed</u>	g<u>a</u>ve	
it's		gr<u>a</u>de	

4. TRICKY WORDS Have students read each row for accuracy, then fluency.

Ⓐ	moved	thought	because	Earth	we're	5
Ⓑ	friends	typed	what	from	would	10

5. MULTISYLLABIC WORDS Have students read the word by parts, tell how many syllables are in the word, then read the whole word.

Ⓐ	u•ni•ted	united	cam•era	camera
Ⓑ	in•ven•tor	inventor	com•put•er	computer
Ⓒ	dif•fer•ent	different	con•ti•nent	continent

6. DICTATION Say the word. Have students say the word, then finger count and say the sounds. Have students say each sound as they touch or write it.

A1 Buildups	**B1** Rhyming Words
c <u>o w</u>	c <u>a m e</u>
<u>s c</u> ow l	n <u>a m e</u>
s c ow l <u>i n g</u>	s <u>a m e</u>

1

PROCEDURES

1. First Reading

Mix group and individual turns, independent of your voice. Have students work toward an accuracy goal of 0–2 errors and practice any difficult words.

2. Second Reading, Short Passage Practice: Developing Prosody

- Demonstrate how to read a line or two with expression. Read at a rate slightly faster than the students' rate. Say something like: Listen as I read the first two sentences with expression and phrasing. I'm going to emphasize certain words and pause between sentences.

  "'We're going to the Bronx!' Ben's dad said. Ben and his brother looked up from the computer."

- Guide practice with your voice. Now read the paragraph with me.

- Provide individual turns while others track with their fingers and whisper read. Provide descriptive and positive feedback.
  [Felix], you read with wonderful expression!

EXTRA PRACTICE 1

Unit 1 Fluency Passage

Name _____

Fluency Passage

My goal is to read with 0–2 errors and ____ words correct per minute.

I read with ____ errors and ____ words correct per minute.

Finding the Bronx

"We're going to the Bronx!" Ben's dad said. Ben and his brother looked up from the computer. Ben's family moved around a lot because of his dad's work. Ben thought it was cool.   12 23 33

"Where on Earth is the Bronx?" Ben asked. He and his brother turned back to the computer. Ben typed in "the Bronx," and the camera zoomed in on a map.   45 57 63

"It looks like it's on the continent of North America, in the United States, near the sea. That's a long way from where we live now!"   76 89

Ben thought about what it would be like at a different school. Ben said to his brother, "We will make lots of friends in the Bronx."   102 115

Homework
I've listened to my child read this passage twice.   Date _____   Signed _____

   2

---

3. Partner Reading: Repeated Reading—Checkout Opportunity

While students do Partner Reading, listen to individuals read the passage. Work on accuracy and fluency, as needed.

4. Homework: Repeated Reading

Have students read the story at home.

EXTRA PRACTICE

Unit 1 Word Fluency A

Name _____

Rhyming Words

High-Frequency Rhyming Words: about, main, rain, train, will, still, bill, hill, red, bed, led, hundred, right, might, night, bright

shout	pout	scout	snout	about
main	rain	train	plain	entertain
will	still	bill	hill	anthill
red	bed	led	shed	hundred
right	might	night	bright	moonlight

Related Words

perfect	perfectly	perfected	perfection	imperfect
inventor	inventors	invented	invention	inventing
science	scientist	scientists	scientific	unscientific
amaze	amazed	amazes	amazing	amazingly
appear	appears	appeared	appearing	appearance

High-Frequency Tricky Words

the	of	a	to	is
a	the	is	of	to
to	is	of	the	a
is	to	the	a	of
of	a	to	is	the

©2009 Sopris West Educational Services. All Rights Reserved.

EXTRA PRACTICE 1

Unit 1 Activity

Name _____

Passage Comprehension
Finding the Bronx

Have students read each sentence or question, then fill in the bubble and/or blank with the correct answer. Think aloud with students and discuss the multiple-choice options, as needed. Remind students to put a period at the end of each sentence.

1. **Who is the story about?**
   ○ Ben and Mike   ● Ben and his family   ○ young boys

2. **Where are Ben and his family moving?**
   ○ Africa   ○ South America   ● the Bronx

3. **Ben and his family are moving because of** his dad's work.
   ● his dad's work   ○ respect   ○ the inventor

4. **In the end, what did Ben say about moving?**
   ○ "Yuck, I don't want to go."
   ○ "The Bronx is a nice place."
   ● "We will make lots of friends in the Bronx."

Paragraph Comprehension

Have students read the paragraph, then fill in the bubble and/or blank for each sentence. Remind them to use a period. Have them read the sentences.

> Yesterday, we used oodles of boxes to pack our belongings. Today, we're driving across the state. Tomorrow, we'll be in our new home.

1. We used oodles of boxes to pack our belongings.
   ● oodles   ○ seven   ○ cram

2. Today , we're driving across the state.
   ○ At noon   ○ Tomorrow   ● Today

3. Tomorrow, we'll be in our new home.
   ○ planet   ● home   ○ car

✓ Check and Correct

©2009 Sopris West Educational Services. All Rights Reserved.   3

PROCEDURES

For each step, demonstrate and guide practice, as needed. Then have students complete the page independently.

1. Activity

Passage Comprehension
- Have students read each question or sentence stem, then fill in the bubble and/or blank with the correct answer.
- Think aloud with students and discuss the multiple-choice options, as needed.
- Remind students to put a period at the end of a sentence.

Paragraph Comprehension
- Have students read the paragraph.
- Have students read each numbered sentence or phrase, then fill in the bubble and blank. Remind them to end sentences with a period, where needed.
- Have students read the completed sentences.

Self-monitoring
Have students read and check their work, then draw a happy face in the Check and Correct circle.

2. Word Fluency (BLMs are located on the CD.)
- To build fluency, have students read Rhyming Words, Related Words, and High-Frequency Tricky Words. Have students read each section three times in a row.
- To build accuracy, have students read all sets with partners.

> **ACCURACY BEFORE FLUENCY**
>
> Word Fluency is designed to build accuracy and fluency. Students should practice for accuracy before working on fluency.

PROCEDURES

1. **Sound Review**

   Use selected Sound Cards from Unit 1.
   - Have students say each sound, building accuracy first, then fluency.
   - Mix group and individual turns, independent of your voice.

2. **Sounding Out Smoothly**
   - For each word, have students say the underlined part, sound out the word smoothly, then read the whole word. (Use the words in sentences, as needed.)
   - Have students read all the words in the row, building accuracy first, then fluency.
   - Repeat practice. Mix group and individual turns, independent of your voice.

3. **Accuracy and Fluency Building**
   - For each task, have students say any underlined part, then read each word.
   - Set a pace. Then have students read the whole words in each task and column.
   - Provide repeated practice, building accuracy first, then fluency.

4. **Tricky Words**

   Have students read each row for accuracy, then fluency.

5. **Multisyllabic Words**

   For each word, have students read each syllable out loud, finger count the syllables, then tell how many syllables are in the word. If needed, use the word in a sentence. Have students read the whole word.

6. **Dictation**

   name, same, save, way, play, today
   - Say "name." Have students say the word. Guide students as they finger count and say the sounds. Have students touch or write the sounds, then read the word.

     The first word is **name.** Say the word. (name)

     Say and count the sounds in **name** with me.

     Hold up one finger for each sound. /nnn/•/āāā/•/m/ How many sounds? (three)

     What's the first sound? (/nnn/) Touch under /nnn/.

     What's the next sound? (/āāā/) Write /āāā/.

     What's the last sound? (/mmm/) Touch under /mmm/.

     Read the word. (name)

     Yes, the Bossy E at the end makes letter a say its name.
   - Repeat with "same" and "save."
   - Continue with the rhyming words: way, play, today.

EXTRA PRACTICE 2

Unit 1 Decoding Practice

Name _____

1. SOUND REVIEW Use selected Sound Cards from Unit 1.

2. SOUNDING OUT SMOOTHLY Have students say the underlined part, sound out and read each word, then read the row.

gr<u>a</u>ss	s<u>o</u>cks	h<u>e</u>lp	fl<u>y</u>

3. ACCURACY/FLUENCY BUILDING Have students say any underlined part, then read each word. Next, have students read the column.

A1 Mixed Practice	**B1** Word Endings	**C1** Rhyming Words	**D1** Buildups
t<u>ea</u>m	<u>scowl</u>s	g<u>ood</u>	v<u>e</u>nt
h<u>igh</u>	scowled	st<u>ood</u>	in<u>ve</u>nt
b<u>all</u>	scowling		<u>invent</u>or
	B2 Shifty Words	f<u>i</u>nd	
sh<u>or</u>ts	sm<u>a</u>ll	k<u>i</u>nd	rise
f<u>ee</u>ls	sm<u>e</u>ll	**C2** Bossy E	sur<u>prise</u>
n<u>ow</u>	sm<u>i</u>le	l<u>i</u>ke	<u>surprise</u>d
<u>air</u>		m<u>a</u>kes	
		h<u>e</u>re	

4. TRICKY WORDS Have students read each row for accuracy, then fluency.

Ⓐ	building	give	everything	everyone	great	5
Ⓑ	thought	learn	does	live	wouldn't	10

5. MULTISYLLABIC WORDS Have students read the word by parts, tell how many syllables are in the word, then read the whole word.

Ⓐ	per•fect	perfect	re•spect	respect
Ⓑ	sec•ond	second	soc•cer	soccer
Ⓒ	real•ly	really	af•ter	after

6. DICTATION Say the word. Have students say the word, then finger count and say the sounds. Have students say each sound as they touch or write it.

A1 Shifty Words	**B1** Rhyming Words
n <u>a</u> m e	w <u>a</u> ~~y~~
<u>s</u> a m e	p l <u>a</u> ~~y~~
s a <u>v</u> e	t o d <u>a</u> ~~y~~

4

PROCEDURES

1. First Reading

Mix group and individual turns, independent of your voice. Have students work toward an accuracy goal of 0–2 errors and practice any difficult words.

2. Second Reading, Timed Reading: Repeated Reading

- Once the group accuracy goal has been achieved, time individual students for 30 or 60 seconds while the other children track with their fingers and whisper read.

- Determine words correct per minute. Record student scores. Celebrate when students reach their goals!

"Wow! [Veronica], you met your goal. That was your best score ever. You get to read to the principal this week."

3. Partner Reading: Repeated Reading (Checkout Opportunity)

While students do Partner Reading, listen to individuals read the passage. Work on accuracy and fluency, as needed.

4. Homework: Repeated Reading

Have students read the story at home.

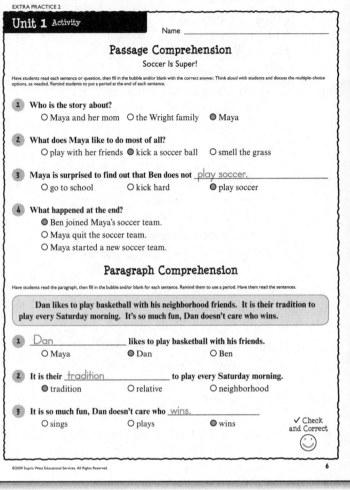

EXTRA PRACTICE

Unit 1 Word Fluency B   Name _____

Rhyming Words

High-Frequency Rhyming Words: now, how, sail, tail, stop, drop, look, took, book, cook

now	how	cow	brow	somehow
sail	tail	rail	trail	pigtail
rug	bug	drug	plug	bedbug
stop	drop	crop	shop	hilltop
look	took	book	cook	cookbook

Related Words

buzz	buzzes	buzzed	buzzing	buzzer
friend	friendly	friendlier	unfriendly	friendship
starve	starves	starved	starving	starvation
breath	breathless	breathe	breathed	breathing
scare	scared	scaring	scary	scarier

High-Frequency Tricky Words

you	was	are	as	his
as	are	his	you	was
his	as	was	are	you
was	you	as	his	are
are	his	you	was	as

EXTRA PRACTICE 2

Unit 1 Activity   Name _____

Passage Comprehension
Soccer Is Super!

Have students read each sentence or question, then fill in the bubble and/or blank with the correct answer. Think aloud with students and discuss the multiple-choice options, as needed. Remind students to put a period at the end of each sentence.

1. **Who is the story about?**
   ○ Maya and her mom   ○ the Wright family   ● Maya

2. **What does Maya like to do most of all?**
   ○ play with her friends   ● kick a soccer ball   ○ smell the grass

3. **Maya is surprised to find out that Ben does not** play soccer.
   ○ go to school   ○ kick hard   ● play soccer

4. **What happened at the end?**
   ● Ben joined Maya's soccer team.
   ○ Maya quit the soccer team.
   ○ Maya started a new soccer team.

Paragraph Comprehension

Have students read the paragraph, then fill in the bubble and/or blank for each sentence. Remind them to use a period. Have them read the sentences.

> Dan likes to play basketball with his neighborhood friends. It is their tradition to play every Saturday morning. It's so much fun, Dan doesn't care who wins.

1. Dan _____ likes to play basketball with his friends.
   ○ Maya   ● Dan   ○ Ben

2. It is their tradition _____ to play every Saturday morning.
   ● tradition   ○ relative   ○ neighborhood

3. It is so much fun, Dan doesn't care who wins.
   ○ sings   ○ plays   ● wins

✓ Check and Correct

PROCEDURES

For each step, demonstrate and guide practice, as needed. Then have students complete the page independently.

1. Activity

Passage Comprehension

- Have students read each question or sentence stem, then fill in the bubble and/or blank with the correct answer.
- Think aloud with students and discuss the multiple-choice options, as needed.
- Remind students to put a period at the end of sentences.

Paragraph Comprehension

- Have students read the paragraph.
- Have students read each numbered sentence or phrase, then fill in the bubble and blank. Remind them to end sentences with a period, where needed.
- Have students read the completed sentences.

Self-monitoring

Have students read and check their work, then draw a happy face in the Check and Correct circle.

2. Word Fluency (BLMs are located on the CD.)

- To build fluency, have students read Rhyming Words, Related Words, and High-Frequency Tricky Words. Have students read each section three times in a row.
- To build accuracy, have students read all sets with partners.

PROCEDURES

1. Sound Review
- Have students say each sound, building accuracy first, then fluency.
- Mix group and individual turns, independent of your voice.

2. Sounding Out Smoothly
- For each word, have students say the underlined part, sound out the word smoothly, then read the whole word. Use the words in sentences, as needed.
- Have students read all the words in the row, building accuracy first, then fluency.
- Repeat practice.

3. Accuracy and Fluency Building
- For each task, have students say any underlined part, then read each word.
- Set a pace. Then have students read the whole words in each task and column.
- Repeat practice.

4. Tricky Words
Have students read each row for accuracy, then fluency.

5. Multisyllabic Words
For each word, have students read each syllable out loud, finger count the syllables, then tell how many syllables are in the word. If needed, use the word in a sentence. Have students read the whole word.

6. Dictation

tank, thank, think, right, light, might
- Say "tank." Have students say the word. Guide students as they finger count and say the sounds. Have students touch or write the sounds, then read the word.

    The first word is **tank.** Say the word. (tank) Say and count the sounds in **tank** with me.

    Hold up one finger for each sound. /t/•/ăăă/•/nnn/•/k/ How many sounds? (four)

    What's the first sound? (/t/) Touch under /t/.
    What's the next sound? (/ăăă/) Write /ăăă/.
    What's the next sound? (/nnn/) Touch under /nnn/.
    What's the last sound? (/k/) Touch under /k/. Read the word. (tank)

- Repeat with "thank" and "think."
- Continue with the rhyming words: right, light, might.

EXTRA PRACTICE 3

Unit 1 Decoding Practice

Name _____

1. SOUND REVIEW Use selected Sound Cards from Unit 1.

2. SOUNDING OUT SMOOTHLY Have students say the underlined part, sound out and read each word, then read the row.

| tr<u>a</u>p | sh<u>ar</u>p | b<u>e</u>st | f<u>ir</u>st |

3. ACCURACY/FLUENCY BUILDING Have students say any underlined part, then read each word. Next, have students read the column.

A1 Sound Practice	B1 Word Endings	C1 Bossy <u>E</u>	D1 Mixed Practice
rock<u>y</u>	stick<u>ing</u>	c<u>a</u>ve	l<u>o</u>ng
might<u>y</u>	find<u>ing</u>	sn<u>a</u>ke	c<u>oo</u>l
hunt<u>er</u>	teach<u>ing</u>	n<u>o</u>se	f<u>oo</u>d
sist<u>er</u>	eat<u>ing</u>	m<u>i</u>ne	m<u>ou</u>th
	smell<u>ing</u>	l<u>i</u>fe	
y<u>ear</u>		h<u>e</u>re	h<u>ar</u>d
m<u>ea</u>t	B2 Buildups		h<u>air</u>
	r<u>e</u>st		h<u>or</u>n
thr<u>ee</u>	int<u>e</u>rest	am<u>a</u>ze	h<u>a</u>ng
t<u>ee</u>th	int<u>e</u>resting	am<u>a</u>zing	

4. TRICKY WORDS Have students read each row for accuracy, then fluency.

| Ⓐ | school | have | two | was | are | 5 |
| Ⓑ | should | work | head | don't | some | 10 |

5. MULTISYLLABIC WORDS Have students read the word by parts, tell how many syllables are in the word, then read the whole word.

Ⓐ	jag·ged	jagged	Chap·man	Chapman
Ⓑ	im·por·tant	important	to·geth·er	together
Ⓒ	a·part·ment	apartment	or·di·nar·y	ordinary

6. DICTATION Say the word. Have students say the word, then finger count and say the sounds. Have students say each sound as they touch or write it.

A1 Shifty Words	B1 Rhyming Words
t <u>a</u> n k	r <u>igh</u> t
<u>th</u> a n k	l <u>igh</u> t
th <u>i</u> n k	m <u>igh</u> t

7

PROCEDURES

1. First Reading

Mix group and individual turns, independent of your voice. Have students work toward an accuracy goal of 0–2 errors and practice any difficult words.

2. Second Reading, Short Passage Practice: Developing Prosody

- Demonstrate how to read a line or two with expression. Read at a rate slightly faster than the students' rate. Say something like: Listen as I read the first two sentences with expression and phrasing. I'm going to emphasize certain words and pause between sentences.

  "I swim in the sea and have sharp jagged teeth and horns on my head. I'm a mighty hunter that eats meat and lives in a rocky cave."

- Guide practice with your voice. Now read the paragraph with me.

- Provide individual turns while others track with their fingers and whisper read. Provide descriptive and positive feedback.
  [Mandy], you read with wonderful expression!

EXTRA PRACTICE 3

Unit 1 Fluency Passage

Name _____

Fluency Passage

My goal is to read with 0–2 errors and ____ words correct per minute.

I read with ____ errors and ____ words correct per minute.

What Am I?

I swim in the sea and have sharp jagged teeth and horns on my head. I'm a mighty hunter that eats meat and lives in a rocky cave.	14 / 28
I'm a kind of fish, but I'm very long and thin like a snake. Some of my brothers and sisters are hard to trap. They are much too big to live in a fish tank.	43 / 58 / 63
I don't have an ordinary nose. Mine looks like two horns sticking out of my head. I can't see very well, so I need this interesting nose for smelling and finding food. My sharp jagged teeth help me trap food in my mouth. I think fish are perfect for eating. What am I? I'm an amazing eel!	75 / 90 / 102 / 116 / 120

Homework
I've listened to my child read this passage twice.   Date _____   Signed _____

8

3. Partner Reading: Repeated Reading (Checkout Opportunity)

While students are Partner Reading, listen to individuals read the passage. Work on accuracy and fluency, as needed.

4. Homework: Repeated Reading

Have students read the story at home.

PROCEDURES

For each step, demonstrate and guide practice, as needed. Then have students complete the page independently.

1. Activity
Passage Comprehension

- Have students read each question or sentence stem, then fill in the bubble and/or blank, or check the blank with the correct answer(s).
- Think aloud with students and discuss the multiple-choice options, as needed.
- Remind students to put a period at the end of sentences.

Paragraph Comprehension

- Have students read the paragraph.
- Have students read each numbered sentence or phrase, then fill in the bubble and blank.
- Have students read the completed sentences.

Self-monitoring

Have students read and check their work, then draw a happy face in the Check and Correct circle.

EXTRA PRACTICE 3

Unit 1 Activity

Name _____

Passage Comprehension
What Am I?

Have students read each sentence or question, then fill in the bubble and/or blank with the correct answer, or make a check mark next to the correct answer. Think aloud with students and discuss the multiple-choice options, as needed. Remind students to put a period at the end of each sentence.

1. What is the passage about?
   - ○ a shark
   - ● an eel
   - ○ a snake

2. Where does an eel swim?
   - ○ in a bottle
   - ○ in a bathtub
   - ● in the sea

3. An eel likes to eat _fish._
   - ● fish
   - ○ seaweed
   - ○ gum drops

4. Check all the things that describe an eel.
   - ✓ long and thin like a snake
   - __ red and white stripes
   - ✓ hunter that eats meat
   - ✓ sharp jagged teeth

Paragraph Comprehension

Have students read the paragraph, then fill in the bubble and/or blank for each sentence. Remind them to use a period. Have them read the sentences.

> Thomas has an amazing fish tank. It is full of cool fish with all kinds of colors. The tank also has a sea horse that likes to hide in the weeds.

1. _Thomas_ has an amazing fish tank.
   - ○ Maya
   - ○ Dan
   - ● Thomas

2. It is full of _cool fish_ with all kinds of colors.
   - ○ cool rocks
   - ● cool fish
   - ○ cool shells

3. The tank also has a _sea horse_ that likes to hide in the weeds.
   - ● sea horse
   - ○ sea weed
   - ○ eel

✓ Check and Correct ☺

9

---

2. Word Fluency (BLMs are located on the CD.)

You may wish to have students repeat practice with Extra Practice, Word Fluency A or B.